HELPING
OTHERS IN
·CRISIS·
ABUSE
FAMILY

KAREN BURTON MAINS

David C. Cook Publishing Co.
Elgin, Illinois—Weston, Ontario

David C. Cook Publishing Co.
Elgin, Illinois—Weston, Ontario
Abuse in the Family
© 1987 David C. Cook Publishing Co.

92 91 90 89   5   4   3   2

Excerpts from the following books are used by permission:

A Betrayal of Innocence, by David B. Peters, © 1986; used by permission of Word Books, publisher, Waco, Texas.

No Place to Hide, by Esther Lee Olson with Kenneth Peterson, © 1982; used by permission of Tyndale House, Wheaton, Illinois.

Child Sexual Abuse: A Hope for Healing, by Maxine Hancock and Karen Burton Mains, © 1987; excerpted with permission of Harold Shaw Publishers, Box 567, Wheaton, Illinois, 60189.

Realities of Child Sexual Abuse, by Nanaimo Rape/Assault Center, Nanaimo, British Columbia; used by permission.

The photographs contained on the cover and throughout this book are stage dramatizations and are for illustrative purposes only. These photographs do not depict actual persons engaged in the situations described in this book, nor are they intended to do so.

Published by David C. Cook Publishing Co.
850 N. Grove Ave., Elgin, IL 60120
Cable address: DCCOOK
Designed by Christopher Patchel
Photo by Bakstad Photographics
Illustrated by Jane Sterrett
Printed in the United States of America
Library of Congress Catalog Card Number 86-72963

ISBN: 1-55513-796-2

To the survivors of abuse who have lived in our home and have allowed us to participate in their healing.

CONTENTS

INTRODUCTION

THE PROBLEM OF ABUSE IN THE FAMILY, IN ALL ITS UGLY forms, is becoming more and more apparent to those of us who are involved in helping hurting people. It is no longer a rare occurrence to have a victim of abuse at our doorsteps or within our congregations. Are we adequately prepared to help these people who often are in crisis situations? I think not. This book is to help inform and equip us for this task. As the problem increases, so must our preparedness.

Consider the experience of Paul Simmons, senior pastor of Ridgeway Avenue Church. This story is one of the case studies that will be examined more closely in Chapter 2. (Names and locations of situations described in this book have been changed to preserve anonymity.) One day the wife of one of his most active, enthusiastic parishioners sat in Simmons's study and unfolded her story of being abused and beaten by her husband.

Paul admits now that his reaction to her story was inadequate. "I truthfully underestimated the seriousness of the violence that was occurring behind the closed doors of the Anderson home," he said. "After praying with Donna, I, in effect, told her to go home and try harder. In the back of my mind, I guess I thought she was exaggerating, or that Neal had really had a bad day, or that beneath that quiet exterior, this woman exercised a gift for making her husband violent. The next time I heard about Donna Anderson, she had been hospitalized due to a severe and life-threatening altercation—Neal had beaten her, then pushed her down their second floor stairs. She was bruised, had sustained several broken ribs, a bad concussion, and internal bleeding.

"These are the moments when you want to turn in your ordination. A sweet woman had come to me for counsel and protection. It had probably been the supreme act of courage in her life. And instead of representing Christ to her, I had allowed all my ignorances, my helplessness, my male prejudice, my own denial—not wanting to think one of my parishioners would act in such a violent way—to prevent me from extending intervention and healing. I could hardly look that woman in the eye when I called on her in the hospital ward, but believe me, I began to learn all I could about the problem of wife abuse in my community.''

Paul Simmons had never before dealt with a wife-battering situation. He was caught unprepared.

My husband and I have had our share of opportunities to help the abused. During the years David and I pastored in inner-city Chicago, we took a young woman into our home. She came to us after two years in a mental hospital—six months of which she had been catatonic. The cause of her psychosis was an incestuous relationship her stepfather had forced on her.

Another young woman who lived with us had spent ten years as a prostitute. To aid healing, I functioned as confessor while she reviewed the horrors of her past. Those terrible, intimate glimpses of sexual abnormality included shadowy memories of early childhood sexual abuse.

We are now involved in a national radio ministry, *The Chapel of the Air*. A letter came to the office from a young woman concerned about losing her mind. Her father had fondled her, had sexual intercourse with her, and said to her, ''What's a father? A father's just a name.''

My husband recently led to the Lord a young man who revealed a history of severe beatings by his father. And I often think of another young man who was introduced to homosexuality by his older brother and humiliated by his father in front of a room full of guests. His pants were stripped from him as a form of punishment and his genitals mishandled. Some part of his psyche froze at six years of age. He was a practicing homosexual until he took his own life while in his 30s.

Within the last year, several close friends have confided to me sudden, overwhelming, surprising memories of long-term sexual abuse, incest, or rape which had been completely locked in their subconscious minds.

After years of speaking and counseling in women's ministries, I have become convinced that an inordinate problem of abuse exists in our culture. Workshops on sexual abuse are packed out; when I mention childhood sexual abuse from the podium, women come to me afterward seeking help from the effects of their past. Another frequent speaker to women's groups and I calculated that as many as one-fourth of the women in our retreats were victims of some kind of abuse.

Here are some statistics for the United States from a variety of sociological sources:

- One out of four girls will be sexually molested by the time she is 18 years old.
- For boys it will be one in ten.
- 80 percent of these abuse victims are mistreated by someone they know and trust.
- In 1976, 413,000 cases of child abuse were reported. By 1981 the count had doubled to 851,000. In 1982, the figures climbed another 12 percent.

This continued exposure through pastoral counseling and itinerant ministry eventually propelled me into a six-month research project in which I read stacks of literature dealing with the topic of abuse in our country, its pervasiveness, its effect on lives, and its cures. This study became a three-week series of radio broadcasts entitled, "Abuse: What We Can Do." Our office was inundated with mail—hundreds of letters from men and women, victims of abuse themselves or writing on behalf of loved ones who had suffered damage from abuse.

The people who wrote us were listeners to Christian radio, people who attended church and considered themselves to be seeking a deeper and more fruitful spiritual life. This substantial voluntary sampling of victims indicated that the abused can be found everywhere—in every level of society, in any geographic location, and, yes, even within the Church.

The Chapel of the Air staff counselor and I spent two months reading and answering letters. At the end of this time I had learned much about the pain and extent of abuse—not just in our nation, but in the very household of God. I was no longer like the woman who said to me, "The media is making such a to-do over the problem of sexual abuse. But I don't know anyone who's been a victim. Do you think this is all being manufactured by the feminists?" The night before, David and I had been awakened by a husband who brought his wife to our home for prayer; she was just beginning to relive memories of early childhood incest.

Education carries the responsibility to educate others. I felt as though I had to become an advocate for those victims of abuse unable to speak for themselves. Surveying the major religious publishers, I discovered that many of them had manuscripts in their publishing schedules dealing with wife battering, child neglect, and incest; but none was planning a book addressed to the survivor of childhood sexual abuse. This became my next project—a book coauthored by Maxine Hancock and myself entitled, *Child Sexual Abuse: A Hope for Healing,* released by Harold Shaw Publishers.

One of the continuing themes found in the stories of these survivors, particularly women, is that pastors and church people often do not know how to respond to revelations of present or past brutality. *The Church Herald* magazine (April 18, 1986) printed the testimony of a woman, married to a battering husband, who sat Sunday after Sunday in the church pew without telling anyone. She never came with black eyes or broken teeth (an abusive male is often deviously clever, inflicting blows to the mid-section of the body, where the damage will not show outwardly). The bruises on her arms were always covered by long-sleeved dresses. But hidden even further from sight were the effects of mental cruelty and sexual abuse. After a number of years the husband left. This woman wrote:

Week after week I sat in church seeking to learn how to be a better, submissive Christian wife so the punishment would stop. I felt trapped by circumstances and by the fact that as a Christian I did not believe in divorce. When, after almost 11 years of marital abuse, my husband left, the church as an institution not only did not offer support, but actually compounded my suffering. A minister implied I was at fault in the divorce and chastised me for voicing my normal feelings of hurt and anger. The consistory (governing body of the church), because they felt inadequate to handle the issue of adultery, chose to ignore it. Finally, when I sought to protect myself and my children by obtaining good legal counsel, the church interpreted this as not being a submissive Christian woman and asked me to refrain from communion because of my "bitter and unchristian spirit."

This testimony of neglect by the Church is most unfortunate but all too frequent. James teaches, "Religion that is pure and undefiled before God and the Father is this: to visit orphans and widows in their affliction . . . ." (James 1:27, RSV). In other words, to be truly Christlike, we must be eager to identify and take care of those who are unprotected, wounded, and without an advocate. The victim of abuse fits this profile.

Part of the reason for Christianity's neglect of the abuse

victim is simply ignorance regarding its occurrence in the local church. Most of us who specialize in women's ministries have met, at an escalating rate, women who share their stories and make us aware how frequently this injustice takes place. More importantly, the research work of Strauss, Gelles, and Steinmetz ("Violence Toward Children in the United States," *American Journal of Orthopsychiatry*, October, 1978) shows that women from *all socioeconomic and religious levels* are abused at similar rates.

The Church must become involved. The professional minister, as well as lay people with ministering hearts, must realize that they are surrounded with some of the most effective tools for helping abuse survivors. Alexander Zaphiris, a well-known medical researcher in this field, maintains in his work *Sexual Abuse of Children: Implications for Treatment* published by Child Protection Division of the American Human Association (1980) that the best hope for incestuous families lies in the efforts of a nonpunitive and cooperative community.

I am convinced this kind of healing community is best formed within a loving, caring, active, informed church which offers discipline, forgiveness, and reconciliation in Christ. Not only can victims in the body of Christ be healed, but outreach can touch others who must cope with the effects of our increasingly violent culture.

Surgeon General C. Everett Koop has called violence America's number-one health problem. This violence includes not only terror on the streets of our cities, but domestic violence that occurs in the privacy of the home. It is a violence which the Church must not ignore.

This book is designed for those in Christian ministry, the youth worker, the pastor, the Christian educator. It is designed to help *you* help the victims of family abuse—those who are in your pews and those who wait outside your doors.

CHAPTER 1

PROFILES OF ABUSE

THE TERM *ABUSE* COVERS A WIDE RANGE OF IMPROPER, injurious activities—wife beatings, sexual molestation, incest, exhibitionism, emotional deprivation, physical neglect. Knowledge of long-term effects of these acts, especially sexual abuse of children, is speculation based on patchwork data. But it is known that personality disorders, psychoses, such as multiple personalities, schizophrenia, and clinical depression can often be directly attributed to an abusive environment.

This book addresses three types of abuse that occur most often in the family—wife battering, abuse of children, and incest.

People who have been victimized by intrafamily abuse often go through life replicating what they experienced. A child whose father beat his mother may often beat his own wife because, for him, that is the normal way for spouses to relate. A woman who was a victim of incest may marry an abusive alcoholic; her subconscious is convinced that this inadequate, needy man is all she deserves. A child deprived of essential emotional and psychological nurturing may withhold this same nurture from his or her own children. Thus, a cycle of abuse goes on.

A victim of an abusive background may also develop physical and psychological disorders—depression, physical disorders, sexual dysfunction, and fears that maim daily living. Mental health experts are beginning to realize that as many as eight out of ten patients with multiple personality disorders had longstanding sexual trauma in their pasts. The emotional and psychological disturbance of the victim is often in proportion to the intensity of the behavioral aberration that caused it.

How widespread is abuse in the home?

No one knows. According to *Time* magazine (September 5, 1983), statistics on private violence are difficult to obtain.

Public violence can be neatly tallied. The FBI is aware of exactly 22,516 murders committed in the U.S. in 1981, a fifth of them killings

13

of loved ones, and that is very close to the true total. But when statisticians turn to private violence, the numbers become iffy, approximate in the extreme. Are there 650,000 cases of child abuse annually, or a million? Or 6 million? Bona fide experts, extrapolating and just guessing, variously cite all those figures and others. . . . It is beyond dispute, however, that extraordinary numbers of women and children are being brutalized by those closest to them.

The dilemma for the victim of abuse has been compounded by a conspiracy of silence regarding family violence. A study noted that if a father commits an offense against someone in his own family, an offense that would label him a "dangerous offender" if committed against a stranger, he will rarely be convicted as a dangerous offender. Judges did not consider an intrafamily offense to be as dangerous as one committed against a stranger's child.

A recent California study estimated that 95 percent of arrested child molesters do not go to prison. Of 30,000 child molesters in California in 1979, only 160 were jailed or hospitalized. Eight out of ten child molesters who were prosecuted were convicted, but nine out of ten child molesters were not prosecuted.

Charges are often dismissed because the child molester is judged to be nonviolent, a first-time offender, or because the family drops the accusations. Usually the only witness is a child whom prosecutors tend to regard as unreliable. Part of the reluctance to prosecute is possibly due to the mistaken attitude that if we don't talk about it, if we don't make waves, the problem will go away.

It is only in recent years that the secular media has focused on the frequent incidence of abuse in our culture. Much of this has been due to female professionals who, since 1970, have listened seriously to women patients. These professionals are largely responsible for exposing the frequency of sexual abuse and bringing it to public attention.

Our silence may also be rooted in denial—we don't want to hear or believe that such things happen. While working with female patients, Sigmund Freud claimed in *Studies on Hysteria* that child sexual trauma was the cause of every case of hysteria. Later he rejected this theory because he was astonished that these children accused their fathers of committing perverse acts against them. Freud wrote, "I was driven to recognize in the end that these reports were untrue and so came to understand that the hysterical symptoms are derived from phantasies and not real occurrences.'' He wrongly concluded that incest could not be that frequent. Thus he developed his explanation of this phenomenon as being due to female ''Oedipal'' complexes. Freud is a major contributor to the conspiracy of silence regarding abuse.

Although precise statistics on family abuse are not available, this chapter will present experts' best estimates on rates of occurrences and general descriptions of wife battering, child abuse, and incest.

Wife Battering

Wife battering is the most frequently occurring form of domestic violence. By definition, wife battering takes place when a husband acts in a physically violent or threatening manner toward his spouse.

Time magazine (September 5, 1983) recorded that six million men in the United States abuse their wives. Although there are incidents of husband batterings (an estimated 282,000 men each year are beaten by their wives), women are the major victims in this literal battle of the sexes.

On December 16, 1986, *World News Tonight*, an ABC TV production, aired a special report on domestic violence in the United States. The report included these two startling statistics: every 18 seconds a wife or girl friend is battered; four are murdered every day.

According to A. R. Denton in *Baker Encyclopedia of Psychology* (Baker Book House, 1985), one out of eight American couples has undergone at least one incident of marital violence. Denton referred to a study that investigated 8,800 divorces. In 90 per cent of those cases, one spouse complained about being physically abused.

In 1979 an FBI study of domestic violence concluded:
- 40 percent of women murdered were killed by their sex partners, and 10 percent of men by theirs.
- 2,000 to 4,000 women were beaten to death that year.
- U.S. police spent one third of their time responding to domestic violence calls. (A 1978 *Police Magazine* article reported that 40 percent of police injuries, and 20 percent of police deaths, were the result of being caught in a family fracas.)
- Battery was the single major cause of injury to women—more significant than auto accidents, rapes, or muggings.

15

A nationwide survey conducted in 1977 by Murray Strauss ("Wife Beating: How Common and Why," *Victimology: An International Journal*, 1977-1978) concluded that 28 percent of the couples in the United States admitted being involved in an ongoing abusive relationship. That figure counted only those willing to tell of their circumstances. The National Institute of Mental Health released findings showing 50 percent of all families in the U.S. were directly affected by domestic violence in some way. Counselor Lenore Walker stated that if you are female, there is one chance in two that you are a battered woman.

The YWCA in the United States has 210 shelter or service programs such as hot lines for battered women, safe-home havens, and counseling centers in 30 states. From 1978 through 1980, the YWCA sheltered 46,000 women and children and gave counseling to 50,000 women, but there is not room to accommodate 80 percent of the women who come to them for assistance.

It used to be assumed that wife beating occurred only among the poor and disadvantaged. More current reports show this assumption to be false. In 1974, for example, police in Fairfax County, Virginia, a wealthy suburb of Washington, D.C., logged 4,073 family disturbance calls. They estimated that 30 assault warrants were requested by wives in that county each week of the year.

Abuse is a crime that knows no religious boundary. *Family Life Today* (December, 1982), a Christian periodical, ran several articles on wife abuse. That issue received overwhelming reader response. An editorial note in a later issue (April, 1983) stated, "The relevancy of this topic to our readership was emphasized by the record number of letters sent to us from Christian women who are or have been victims of wife abuse . . . more than we have ever received in response to an article in the magazine."

Many evangelical Christians find it hard to believe that wife battering can take place in a Christian home. "It's a sordid situation, I agree," commented one pastor. "And I don't doubt for a minute that it does exist. But not in my congregation. I would guess that wife abuse is very rare in the evangelical community."

Daniel Keller, an evangelical pastor in Indianapolis, Indiana, has a different experience. "From talking with my fellow pastors in the area, I would estimate that 10 percent of the couples in most evangelical congregations are involved in abusive relationships. I see a new case of wife battering on the average of once every month or so within my congregation," he says. "These are middle-class church couples—generally professing Christians with conservative Christian upbringings."

Abuse occurs when a woman is subjected to recurrent forceful physical or psychological attacks. Injuries from physical abuse may be as mild as bruises and cuts, or as serious and potentially lethal as broken bones and teeth, ruptured organs, miscarried pregnancies, and bullet or stab wounds. An abusive husband may push, slap, bite, kick, choke, hit, throw objects at, rape, or force sadistic sexual acts upon his wife. He may threaten her with a weapon, confine her against her will, or destroy her personal property.

In an abusive relationship neither partner deserves 100 percent of the blame. Each situation is different, requiring individual evaluation. A variety of causes and contributing factors may be found. Some husbands may become abusive infrequently, triggered only by unusual circumstances; others may be abusive anytime something displeases them.

Profile of a Wife Batterer

What kind of a man would abuse his wife?

There is good statistical evidence to assume that he was beaten as a child. Abusive behavior is often learned through experience. As a result, the abusive male may have suffered emotional damage during his developmental years that can hinder adult maturation.

Michael Groetsch, director of probation for the New Orleans Municipal Court, works with accused wife abusers every week and recognizes their arrested development. "There is a very interesting analogy between a male batterer and a two- or three-year-old child. His tantrums are very similar to those of a two-year-old. Like a narcissistic child, the batterer bites when he's throwing a tantrum. I have seen many women come in with teeth marks all over their arms and legs."

Because the abuser suffers low self-esteem, he will often select a mate with the same characteristic. Since the wife usually sees herself as having little value, the husband is unable to receive the emotional support from her that he needs. This feeds

17

his perception that his wife is uncaring and needs to be controlled. The batterer is likely to manifest drastic mood swings—from warm and charming to outraged and vicious. He will commonly be extremely jealous.

A. R. Denton wrote in *Baker Encyclopedia of Psychology* (Baker Book House, 1985) that the child who grew up in an abusive home has learned to use violence to gain personal freedom. The male child will tend to adopt an attitude of superiority and control over females in the home.

An abusive man is likely to be outgoing and charming, but he is often extremely insecure. He usually has an obsessive need to control his wife, to keep her close, to own her. Those who admit to being violent frequently blame the woman for causing him to be abusive. As one man who was quoted in *Time* magazine (September 5, 1983) stated, "Most of the time, I thought I was right. It [the violence] was called for."

The abusive husband desperately needs to be in charge. He has wrongly learned that to be masculine is to be violent. He equates masculinity and headship with the use of physical strength. Distorted traditional views of marital sex roles lend support to his use of force. When this man hears he should be the authority at home, he expects everything to go his way. He wants the last word in every discussion; he wants to make all the decisions. Physical violence seems justified to him when he needs help in maintaining this level of authority. This man perceives abuse as normal male behavior. Telling a woman she must submit to this kind of treatment is like telling the wife of an alcoholic she must keep the cupboard stocked with alcohol because her husband has a drinking habit.

In almost every instance, outside intervention is needed to stop the abuse. Even if confronted by family or friends about his need for treatment, few violators will stay in a treatment program without a court order. They must have help to become aware of their misperception of male/female relationships. In order to change their behavior pattern, they need help to see that violent behavior is abnormal. The *World News Tonight* report referred to earlier stated that if the violator would be arrested after the first offense, it would greatly decrease the likelihood that he or she would repeat abusive incidents. The psychological dynamics in abusive relationships make it difficult for the victim to press charges against the spouse. Success in legally charging the offender is made more difficult in some states (like Pennsylvania), because the law states the incident must be witnessed.

The battering process seems to follow a cycle: first a buildup of tension, then a violent explosion, and finally a period of remorse and apologies that rekindle hope that the batterer will change as he promises over and over to become a loving, stable adult.

It *is* possible to change the profile of an abusive man. In a workshop in Rockland County, New York, a chronic wife batterer reported after completing therapy, "If a husband takes control of himself, a wife cannot make him hit her."

Profile of a Battered Wife

What kind of woman would subject herself to such treatment?

The classic abused wife may seem to be the epitome of society's traditional values. She is submissive and religious, a woman who follows where her husband leads. Her marriage is the most important thing in her life, and she is completely devoted to her home and family. She shares the view of some women, particularly ultraconservative Christian women, that the female is innately inferior to the male.

A wife who is battered is generally not "liberated" or headstrong. She does not usurp her husband's authority. She would do anything, even sacrifice her own bodily health and mental well-being, to make her marriage last. But, like her husband, she suffers from low self-esteem. This prevents her from affirming and nurturing him, with the result that she can appear cold and rejecting. Yet, in spite of being abused by her husband, she will often protect him, refusing to press charges against him.

Child Abuse

Child abuse in the home can take two forms—physical abuse or child battering, and parental neglect. Child battering usually produces evidence that is outwardly visible on the child's body. Neglect is more difficult to identify. It often does not show physically until it has gone on for an extended period of time.

Physical Abuse

Richard J. Gelles, who wrote in the *American Journal of Orthopsychiatry*, October, 1978, defined violence as "an act carried out with the intention, or perceived intention, of physically injuring another person." Gelles stated that estimates of "truly battered children," based on projections from regional, state, city, or agency samples, vary from 30,000 to 1.5 million each year. Annual estimates of children beaten to death by relatives or guardians vary from 700 to 2,000.

Gelles conducted a study of family violence based on anonymous self-reporting. Admitting the difficulties with this kind of research, he nevertheless concluded the data suggested from 900,000 to 1.8 million American children between the ages of three and seventeen had had a parent use a gun or knife on them.

The National Center on Child Abuse and Neglect reported that a minimum of 625,000 children are abused and neglected in the United States each year. This figure is considerably lower than the generally accepted estimate of one million or more incidents annually, but this particular NCCAN study concerned itself only with children who suffered demonstrable signs of physical or emotional injury. This estimate of 625,000 cases translates into an annual rate of 10.5 maltreated children for every 1,000 children under the age of 18.

One thing is certain: the number of reported cases of child battering in the United States is rising sharply. The increasing figures may not represent an actual increase in incidents of abuse, but more willingness to report suspected abuse. A 1970 poll showed that about ten percent of Americans considered child abuse a serious national problem. A recent Louis Harris survey revealed that this figure had increased to 90 percent. Children who are severely beaten or murdered by their parents are the focus of media coverage nearly every day. This attention has resulted in educating the public to the severity and frequency of the problem of physical child abuse.

Child Neglect

Child neglect is a subtle, less obvious, slower form of abuse. This type of abuse has been virtually ignored by the Church, despite the fact it is reported more frequently to authorities and accounts for more deaths than physical violence.

Neglect includes emotional, physical, nutritional, and psychological deprivation. The neglectful parent is one who is careless about nurturing, who is ill equipped to protect, and who has few, if any, parenting skills. Often this parent was raised in a neglectful environment as well.

According to 1981 statistics of National Study on Child Neglect and Abuse Reporting, only four out of every 100 abused children in the United States who were reported had experienced major physical injury. But 60 out of every 100 reported children experienced a type of physical neglect. Furthermore, major physical injury was associated with 34 percent of child deaths reported in 1981, but neglect was associated with 56 percent.

Robert Burgess, while conducting studies on neglectful family units (*The Dilemma of Child Neglect: Identification and Treatment*, American Human Association Children's Division, 1983), found that these families interacted less with each other than emotionally healthier family units. When they did interact, the contacts were more negative. A negative contact is one which communicates derogatory or demeaning statements and/or gestures. Neglectful mothers and fathers directed positive behavior toward their children at a rate approximately 50 percent lower than other families; neglectful mothers displayed rates of negative behavior twice as high as other mothers. Neglectful fathers exhibited negative behavior 75 percent more than other fathers.

Profile of an Abused Child

The abused child will display negative behavior nearly 50 percent more often than the children in healthier families, according to data gathered in 1982 by the National Study on Child Neglect and Abuse Reporting. If tested, this child will score significantly lower than his or her peers in nearly all developmental areas. The neglected children may even score lower than an abused child. The greatest deficit was in language development.

What is usually considered normal behavior for children may be seen excessively in a neglected child. He or she may wiggle, fiddle with objects, interrupt, tease, cry and whine, distract easily, have intense emotional responses and tantrums. This child may be physically and verbally aggressive. He or she may be defiant and, at the same time, demand excessive amounts of adult attention. In addition, an abused child may destroy objects on purpose, tell lies, be fearful, moody, and take an "I can't" approach to tasks. The list can go on.

Researchers have concluded that neglect can be called "the creepy-crawly" killer of children. This means that, while it occasionally leads to physical death, neglect frequently inhibits growth and development of a child to his or her maximum potential. This child truly needs the intervention of a concerned, caring outsider.

Incest

Experts define incest as sexually arousing incidents between family members (except between husband and wife), whether there is a blood relationship or not. Health researchers and mental health professionals prefer to use the term *intrafamily child sexual abuse* (ICSA).

Every state in the U.S. has laws against child sexual abuse with its own legal definition. Sexual abuse may be defined as the use of a child for sexual gratification or allowing a child to be used by others. Legal definitions may include sexual intercourse, fondling, sexual verbal abuse, obscene telephone calls, forcing a child to watch sexual acts, exhibitionism, voyeurism, and child pornography.

How widespread is incest? Again, no one knows. Because these acts occur in private, and because the victim has been coerced and/or threatened if he or she reports the incident, nobody knows how frequently ICSA occurs. One researcher stated that for every case reported, perhaps as many as 20 cases go unreported. Another estimated that as many as ten million Americans from every cultural, economic, geographic, racial, and religious background may be involved in incest.

Dr. Vincent De Francis launched a three-year study of child sexual abuse in New York City. His study, reported in *Protecting the Child Victim of Sex Crimes* (American Humane Association, 1965) and funded in part by a grant from the United States Children's Bureau, yielded astonishing findings. Much of the following data from this pioneer research has been validated by subsequent studies:

1. It is probable that incidence of sexual abuse in children may be many times larger than the reported incidence of physical abuse.

2. In 41 percent of the cases, offenses were repeated over periods of time ranging from weeks to seven years.

3. Most offenders were males ranging in age from 17 to 68.

4. In 75 percent of the cases the offender was known to the child and/or to the child's family. Only 25 percent were alleged to be strangers.

5. Victims ranged in age from infancy to 16. The median age was 11. The ratio of victims was ten girls to one boy.

In "Hidden Victims: the Facts About Incest" (*His* magazine, April, 1983), Dr. Richard Butman, a Christian psychologist, wrote, "Despite the clear prohibition of incest in Leviticus 18: 6-18, the majority of reported aggressors are regular church attenders. It is difficult to measure someone's 'Christianity,' but researchers report that the adult males tend to be very devout, moralistic, and conservative in their religious beliefs."

Again, the data are extremely sketchy, but I, like others who are involved in helping heal the effects of incest, regularly hear stories of ICSA implicating minister fathers, missionary grandfathers, and churchgoing dads with such regularity that we can only cry, "Help! Oh, God, help us!"

Strangely enough, secrecy often binds the victim of sexual abuse to the abuser. Incest, in particular, is much more than the violation of a child's body. It betrays the trust of a child. The victim's loyalty and love for the abuser can make it difficult for him or her to speak up. If the victim does find the courage to tell a friend, relative, or professional such as a teacher or minister, the listener may react to this revelation with disbelief, judgment, or denial. This type of reaction increases the emotional injury already done to the child.

The adult who makes sexual advances to a child has used his or her authority as a wedge to avow the child to secrecy and silence. The child might be told, "Your mother will leave us if she finds out," or "If you tell anyone, they will put me in jail, and it will be your fault," or "I'll kill you if you tell anyone," or "This is our special game; it's a secret between you and me."

The child complies out of obedience and reverence for the adult position. As one victim of incest states, "It's strange, isn't it? As a child you feel like you don't have any right to question what an adult is doing. You are brought up to respect adults and think that they know what is best. I found myself saying, 'Well, I guess it must be okay. . . . He's a grown-up.' " This compliance may be increased if the child considers the abuser to be a Christian.

As with other forms of abuse, incest tends to affect lifelong behavior patterns of the victim. David B. Peters wrote in *A Betrayal of Innocence*:

Perhaps the most important single difference we see between the effects of child sexual abuse on female victims and those on male victims is the tendency of the male victim to become a victimizer. It is becoming increasing clear as we study this problem that the female victim tends to victimize herself as the result of having been sexually abused. The negative self-image, developed as the result of her molestation, is acted out in such ways as to invite others to punish her for what she perceives as her own shortcomings.

Profile of an Incestuous Family

According to L. N. Ferguson (*Baker Encyclopedia of Psychology*, Baker Book House, 1985, p. 567), five factors may characterize a family in which incest occurs.

One factor is the family dynamic. Poor communication patterns, unhealthy alliances, inadequate methods of handling conflict, and dependency are seen. A second factor is the inability to deal with sexual issues and intimacy. In many cases the strongly religious homes have more difficulty talking about sexuality. Needs or urges are not discussed. Behaviors begin subtly and remain hidden. A third factor is a strong authoritarian milieu as found in many religious homes. The men in the families believe they "own" their women. The fourth factor is the unconscious dynamic of unresolved hostilities or wishes toward parents. Coming from a family where incest occurred, either as a victim or a witness, may predispose the person to unhealthy interaction patterns with a spouse or children that reflect anger, fear, or distrust. A fifth factor is the emotional immaturity and poor impulse control often noted in the men who commit incest.

The Church's Role

These three kinds of abuse comprise a vicious triad. Sexual abuse and physical abuse usually coexist within a family unit. Both are often preceded by emotional neglect.

Most abusive parents love their children very much but not very well. The majority of these abusers were abused themselves as children. For many, abusive behavior is the only style of parenting they know. Abused children grow up to be abusive adults. This cycle is ongoing because 95 percent of child abusers become parents who, by example, teach their children to abuse. Unless confession, repentance, forgiveness, and reconciliation take place, the sins of the father are visited upon their children to the third and fourth generations (Ex. 34: 7).

Since abuse is usually cyclical, consider the multiplication factor of abuse: a mother abuses her four children who grow up (if they live) to become abusive parents. And so it goes. The effects of the epidemic of abuse on our culture is devastating. A study among prostitutes revealed that at least half of their initial sexual experiences were with their own fathers. Studies of prison populations show that more than 90 percent of all inmates claim to have been abused as children.

A victim of incest told me that years later she had confronted the violator. He confessed and repented. She said, "I have great hope for him. But I also know, that through my actions, I am breaking the cycle of sexual abuse. This is a condition that, through the power of Christ, I am not going to allow to continue in my own little family."

Time magazine (September 5, 1983) called child abuse the ultimate betrayal. I agree. The parent, whose role is to nurture, protect, shelter, and love the child, becomes the victimizer. *Time*'s article asked, "If wolves and bears and birds take meticulous care of their young, why are human beings subjecting theirs to whippings and punches and sexual perversions?"

The answer, of course, is spiritual: the human heart is capable of evil. This truism is fundamental to Scripture. Humanity is inherently different from animals by design of our Creator. Having been fashioned in His image, we have the capacity for great goodness. But because of the Fall and its universal effect on people, we also have the capacity for great injustice. Perhaps we can see no better evidence of our dark capabilities than in the study of abuse of an innocent child in his or her own home.

Another fundamental message of Scripture is that Christ is capable of redeeming the evil hearts of men and women. This Christ is familiar with abuse. He was stripped, beaten, mocked, humiliated, scourged, and lifted up naked to die a tortuous death. He is the same Christ who was an advocate of children. ". . . But whoever causes one of these little ones who believe in me to sin, it would be better for him to have a great millstone fastened around his neck and to be drowned in the depth of the sea. See that you do not despise one of these little ones; for I tell you that in heaven their angels always behold the face of my Father who is in heaven. So it is not the will of my Father who is in heaven that one of these little ones should perish" (Matthew 18:6, 10, 14, RSV).

The ability to break the abuse cycle is needed, but the world cannot provide it. This is one purpose of the Church in society. Judgment? Yes. Conviction of guilt? Yes. But foremost, forgiveness, release, and redemption. "For God sent the Son into the world, not to condemn the world, but that the world might be saved through him" (John 3:17, RSV). The Church must offer healing, support, and a loving community. There must be holy men and women, empowered by the living Christ, who are not afraid to walk into the hells of others' lives so that the abused, as well as the abusers, can be set free.

CHAPTER 2

CASE STUDIES OF ABUSE

S IN OF ANY KIND IS A FORM OF ABUSE—ABUSE OF GOD, abuse of others, abuse of self. Because of our sinful nature, each of us is guilty of abuse in varying degrees. We need to keep this in mind as we examine three cases of blatant abuse. In spite of our own propensity to sin, it can be easy to develop a judgmental or condemning attitude toward the abuser.

Here are the experiences of Donna, a battered wife, Timothy, an abused child, and Nancy, a victim of incest. These stories can help us see that the Christian—related to the redemptive Christ, believing in the renewing power of the Holy Spirit, attempting to live a life of love and holiness before a righteous God—has the tools to bring healing and hope to the abused. These stories have been altered to preserve the anonymity of the victims, but the events are true.

Donna Anderson—A Battered Wife

Rev. Paul Simmons, senior pastor of Ridgeway Avenue Church, saw Donna Anderson Sunday after Sunday, yet he didn't *really* see her until she had been coming to church for a year and a half. He had noticed her husband Neal, though, right away.

Neal was the exuberant life of every church social. His bountiful good humor, uproarious repartee, and zest for life drew people's attention. Donna basked quietly in the overflow of attention given Neal. Soft-spoken and undemanding, she was a pleasant woman who seemed to adore her husband.

Donna became the center of Pastor Simmons's attention one afternoon as she sat in his office. Her eyes filled with tears as she stammered out a story he could scarcely believe. She parted her hair to show where Neal had yanked out a chunk and rolled up a sleeve to reveal dark bruises on her upper arm. She was afraid for her own safety and that of the children because Neal had threatened her with a gun. Declaring her love for Neal, she felt helpless to stop his continual brutality. He might kill her if he knew she had come to Simmons's office. But she needed help and knew of no other place to turn.

Paul Simmons could not reconcile the two images of Neal Anderson—the charming, witty public personality and this allegedly abusive, violent, private man. He could not believe that Donna was relating an accurate picture of their life together. As a result, after praying with her, Paul sent her back home—only to be battered some more.

The next time the pastor saw Donna, she was in a hospital bed having been severely beaten by Neal. After battering her, he pushed her down a flight of stairs. She suffered from a concussion, broken ribs, internal bleeding, and multiple bruises.

Paul Simmons realized he had acted improperly and out of ignorance. He knew he had to learn more about domestic violence. Very soon he realized that Neal Anderson fit perfectly the typical profile of a battering husband. Simmons watched the way secular professionals worked on the Anderson case as a result of Donna's hospitalization. These people took her situation seriously. They treated Neal as the lawbreaker that he was—a man guilty of assault. A legal restraining order was taken out against him; it explained that he could be prosecuted for violent behavior toward his wife.

Donna was informed of her legal options. She requested that a caseworker from the nearby battered wives shelter be assigned to work with her and Neal. These actions applied pressure to Neal, helping him realize his need for weekly family counseling. During this time he was not allowed to live in the home.

Pastor Paul Simmons, a humble man, admitted he had been wrong in his initial conclusions about Donna and in the approach he had used with her. To better equip himself to help others like Donna, he spent time at the battered wives shelter talking with residents and social workers. He discovered that, like himself, the medical profession and social agencies are sometimes contributors to the battering syndrome. One worker said, "They [uninformed professionals] treat the women like they are crazy." Doctors frequently fail to note signs of abuse, labeling battered women psychotic or hypochondriacal, prescribing tranquilizers, and telling them to go back home. As a result these women often come to doubt their sanity.

Rev. Simmons offered a room in his church as a regular

meeting place for group therapy sessions for battering husbands. He became a friend to the men, most of whom never attended church. One of the men frequently greeted him with a cheerful "Hi-yah, Rev!"

While listening in on one of the sessions, at the suggestion of the therapist, Paul began to realize that his own father had used abusive discipline methods on him—beating him with a belt and frequently shutting him in a closet. Paul was surprised to discover that he had an active, hidden fear of his father even though his father was now elderly and feeble. Paul could vividly recall weeping as a young boy, pleading to be let out of the closet. As he reflected, Paul was able to admit to himself that he, too, had frequently used excessively strong disciplinary methods on his own children. He could remember struggling to keep control of himself in family crises. He had vowed he would never use violence on his children. Paul testified how easily an abused child could become an abusive adult.

After listening to that therapy session, Paul began to wonder if his own proclivity to violence had allowed him to turn a deaf ear to Donna's plea for help. She had reminded him of a past he preferred to forget.

Donna and Neal are together now although their relationship is shaky. There are frequent difficult moments; a couple have required outside intervention. But Paul Simmons believes that there is hope for this couple, and he prays that their marriage will soon become healthy.

Simmons has learned a great deal. He is changing his approach to the subject of domestic abuse. He is now developing strategy for intervention, improving his counseling skills, and establishing a theology regarding an ethical and pastoral perspective toward abuse.

He says, "I realize that all the relational verses in Scripture that teach us how to care [for] and love one another are also applicable to the Christian family. In my teaching and preaching, I try to show my people how they can live out these truths in their personal lives. Also, I suppose I've heard hundreds of sermons on 'wives, submit yourselves to your husbands,' and I have preached a few myself. But I have never heard one on Colossians 3:19, 'Husbands . . . do not be harsh with [your wives].' Do not kick, bite, punch, strike, pummel, push, etc., etc. I preached a sermon on that recently. This is one way I can provide a deterrent to those males who are borderline abusers. In another way, it is a means by which I can educate my congregation to the real difficulty of abuse which exists in our contemporary culture.''

Timothy Martin—A Neglected Child

Timothy Martin drove Sunday School teachers to distraction. He was whiny, inattentive, and did not know how to relate to other children in class. He provoked incidents and then complained that his classmates were unfair to him. He defied rules, but also demanded teacher Pat Meyer's attention. His emotions were mercurial—raucous laughter one moment and a flood of tears the next. He often looked as though he had dressed himself without supervision.

When Pat investigated Timothy's family, she was not surprised to learn that his parents never came to church. A next-door neighbor, Annie Shoreham, who had attended the church for years, had been bringing him with her. She said to Pat, ''I know he's a handful, but oh, my dear, if you could see his home!''

Pat Meyer discovered that Timothy's mother, Alice, was an alcoholic. She would begin drinking early in the afternoon, be inebriated by the time the children arrived home from school, but still be able to fix supper and carry on a conversation. Alice would not admit to having a drinking problem. She hid her supply of alcohol as well as much of the family's meager household allowance to replenish her supply.

When Alice was on an alcoholic binge, Timothy's 12-year-old sister, Maureen, kept the family functioning to the best of her preteen ability. The father, John, was still supplying the family with an adequate income. But his frustration was mounting as the family seemed to be more and more disorganized—a dirtier house, mounting unpaid bills, an increasingly difficult relationship with his wife and children. John's mounting anxiety and tension were expressed in explosions of rage and more frequent absences from the family. As Pat suspected, Timothy was often left to fend for himself.

Some weeks earlier Annie Shoreham had begun to notice Timothy because no one seemed to like him or play with him. One winter day he played in the snow wearing a thin sweater and no gloves. He seemed to be relegated to the outside world when most children were inside watching television. One day she watched as Alice shooed him outside, stumbled on the porch steps to collect the mail, and then ranted at Timothy as though he had caused her misstep.

Annie had needed someone to love and Timothy needed to be loved. She had invited him in for hot chocolate and asked if he would like to help her make cookies. Soon there was more flour on the table and cupboards than in the bowl, but the old woman and the young child were happy. Each had found a friend.

Annie began to bring him to church, inviting him over early enough to feed him scrambled eggs, bacon, and biscuits. She enjoyed the solace of her Sunday School class for seniors so much that she thought a class for Timothy might offer him some of the nurture missing from his life. She prayed the class would be taught by someone with love, compassion, and lots of creative resources.

Pat Meyer was everything Annie hoped she would be. She was a doer who loved to help people. Providentially, she had a background that helped her understand the family system that surrounds chemically dependent people. Pat's father had been alcoholic, and she remembered the embarrassment and pain of growing up in a home like Timothy's.

One afternoon Pat called on Timothy's family. Mom was "sick," but she talked with Maureen. The girl was pretty, but she showed signs of being frazzled around the edges and slightly defensive when Pat asked how she could get in touch with Timothy's father. Pat left her phone number with the Martins.

Pat was surprised when the father called her that same evening. During their conversation, Pat prayed fervently under her breath for God's guidance. Out of that conversation, a network of help for the family began to grow. This network was made up of interested people from the church, teachers at school, counselors with a local Al-Anon/Alateen Family Group (which works with families of alcoholics), and Annie Shoreham. Annie had come to be a substitute grandma for Timothy. Her house became a haven for him when things got too rough in his own home.

John Martin grew to trust the concerned intervention of Pat Meyer. She would stop by to say to him, "I just wanted to tell you the darling thing Timothy said in church this morning. . . " John felt support from Pat because she could truthfully say, "I understand."

In time, Timothy's father and sister began to attend Pat Meyer's church. This led to their personal acceptance of Jesus Christ as Savior.

Through the assistance of a professional chemical-dependency counselor who specialized in working with families like Timothy's, Alice was pressed to begin to recognize her problem. John, Maureen, and in his own way, young Timothy learned not to lie about Alice's alcohol habit. Together they worked their way out of emotional dependency and a sense of shame that often characterize families like theirs. In time, Mrs. Martin began substance-abuse counseling. This came only after the family learned to let her face some of the consequences of her alcohol dependency—including loss of esteem in the eyes of friends, outsiders taking over her mothering responsibilities, knowledge within her extended family of her inability to cope with life, and hearing her family speak the truth about her condition.

The key to this progress was a small group of committed people who met regularly to plan how to help the Martins. Did Timothy need a warm winter coat? Could some of the demands of family life be taken from Maureen? What did John need? Should he be included in a men's Bible study, the bowling league, or the fall inquirer's class that met with the pastor? Who would talk to Timothy's teacher and Maureen's school counselor about the children's progress in the classroom?

Pat Meyer knew the risks of interfering in a family that might refuse her help. But because her experiences had convinced her that abused children deserve an advocate and that unhealthy families can be restored, she was prompted to act. She also knew that trusting in Christ was essential for wholeness for the Martin family; it had made such a difference in her own healing. She was convinced that Timothy was in her Sunday School class, not by chance, but because her sovereign God knew she would be able to show love to Timothy and his family.

Nancy Winchell—A Victim of Incest

During Communion one Sunday morning, Nancy Winchell began to sob. Then her shoulders heaved. Doris McCracken exchanged places with her husband and put her arms around the crying woman. Dan McCracken dug a clean linen handkerchief out of his pocket and passed it down the pew.

"I feel like I need to vomit," whispered Nancy and the two women made their way out of the pew to the washroom. There Doris heard dry retching sounds from one of the stalls.

Nancy thanked Doris for her care but made her way quickly out of the church before the benediction was given. She was obviously embarrassed to have been a source of commotion.

The next day Doris received a call from Nancy who hesitantly expressed a desire to have lunch together. When the women met, Nancy said, "I have such a terrible time at Communion." When Doris asked why, Nancy said she felt like such a wretched sinner. Finally Nancy revealed a story so painful that Doris wondered how she could have kept it inside her so many years.

When Nancy was a child, her father had frequent intercourse with her. He had forced oral sex on her, linking it to a ritualistic, occult "eucharist." Later Nancy became a Christian, but she still had many struggles. One was trying to get over the extreme nausea she felt whenever she participated in the Lord's Supper. In her mind, the ceremony was linked with her father's blasphemous, abusive behavior.

Nancy was 28. She had been married, then divorced. Because she had been treated for chronic manic-depression, her former husband had been awarded custody of their son. Nancy was overweight, prone to mood swings, unable to hold a job for long, and had an overwhelming need to control her environment. Her former husband had complained that she "manipulates like crazy." He did not want to live with her moodiness, her adamant strong will, and her apparent need to run his life.

After the divorce, Nancy had begun seeing a Christian counselor. At the therapist's suggestion, Nancy began attending a women's Bible study. She soon recognized that she couldn't live any longer without Christ. In faith, she committed herself to Him.

While in therapy her first recollections of incest surfaced in her dreams. But as she continued therapy, she began to experience horrifying memories. From earliest childhood she had been sexually victimized by her father, an older brother, and an uncle.

A psychiatrist began to help her recount these memories of the past. She seemed to relive each experience as it was released from the subconscious vault where it had been stored. (This aspect of therapy will be covered more completely in the next chapter.)

The painful memories came most frequently at night. Nancy needed loving friends who would not abandon her as she went through this emotional crisis. Bonnie Criswell, one of the women in the Bible study who knew Nancy's story, invited Nancy to live in her home until the worst memories had been faced. Bonnie was not trained in psychology but had a nursing background, as well as an abundance of compassion. She was able to be calm and supportive when Nancy faced horrendous memories.

Bonnie and Nancy closely communicated with the psychologist. He explained that healing could not occur until the past had been reviewed. He also made himself available for phone consultation if a memory seemed unbearable.

Doris McCracken also had remained an important person in Nancy's life. Since the time Nancy revealed her story, Doris had extended warmth and love to the struggling woman. In a sense, she became a substitute for Nancy's own mother. Nancy had many negative feelings toward her mother because she had never tried to intervene to prevent Nancy from being sexually violated. Once, in fact, when young Nancy had tried to get her mother to protect her, the woman had refused and said, "If you have trouble, it's because you ask for it."

Doris and Dan McCracken showed Nancy what a healthy, loving, Christian family was like. This was important because Nancy had begun to suspect that all family relationships were as horrendous as her own.

One evening, Nancy shared her psychological journey and some of her experiences with the six women in her Bible study, all of whom had become close friends and desired to help bear each other's burdens. One of the women felt Nancy's experience had been demonically influenced because of her father's interest in the occult. She suggested that the group pray that she would be freed from the bondage of her family's incestuous acts. They laid hands on Nancy and asked for her to be freed from any evil influence brought against her by her father, mother, brother, or uncle. Then they asked God to allow His love to flow into every part of Nancy. When they finished, Nancy spontaneously hugged each woman. This in itself was a manifestation of God's love, since she usually had tried to avoid physical contact.

Later Doris suggested that Nancy should go to her pastor and tell him about the occult associations that made taking Communion such an ordeal for her. Nancy said she could not possibly tell her horrible story, but Dan and Doris offered to go with her when she was ready. Finally, Nancy agreed. After she finished telling him about her past, the pastor said, "You know, Nancy, you were not responsible for those terrible acts that were done to you. You were an innocent child."

The minister asked Nancy if she had forgiven the people who had so misused her. Tearfully she replied that she had tried. The McCrackens, the paster, and Nancy, knelt as Nancy began to pray for forgiveness for those who had abused her. When she was done, the pastor said, "When we forgive like this, we know what it means to be [like] Christ who forgave us all our sins and died so that we might be freed from the effects of our own sins and the effects of other's against us."

Then he took the elements for Communion which he kept in small containers for use when visiting the sick. Smiling as he turned to Nancy, he said, "I wonder if you would allow me to serve you Communion. Actually I would be giving you the elements in the place of Christ, and it would be a great privilege if I could serve you privately—you Nancy, and Dan and Doris— here in my study." For the first time in her Christian life, Nancy received the elements of the Lord's Supper without a wave of nausea.

On hearing Nancy's story, a counselor said, "That is an ideal model for healing. If we could establish those kinds of caring communities, hundreds of people could be helped. A psychologist, or a social worker can't possibly do it all."

This "wonderful model" can be found in the community of Christ. The healing potential of the Church in our broken, violence-torn world is enormous.

CHAPTER 3

QUESTIONS THE ABUSED MAY ASK

VICTIMS OF ABUSE, ESPECIALLY CHILDREN, RARELY VERBAL-ize questions about being abused unless encouraged to do so. A therapist from the Child Sexual Abuse Treatment and Training Center in Bolingbrook, Illinois, was asked, "What questions does an abused child or a victim of incest ask?" His terse reply: "They don't." An adult often becomes aware of sexual abuse, the therapist explained, by observing odd behavior on the part of the child.

One young boy, for example, was observed licking a mirror. When asked why he was doing that, he said, "That's what my daddy makes me do to him." Such abused children usually don't ask questions until they have been in therapy for some time.

When victims of domestic violence—wife battering, child abuse, and incest—do have questions, they often ask them indirectly. A child is likely to make a statement that gives oblique information. He or she might say, "I don't like Uncle Tom." Or the child might tell you about a friend to whom a boy had done "bad things." The sensitive adult should probe statements like these, gently and without pressure. Generally a child who has offered this much information wants to offer more and will respond to compassionate questioning. Follow-up questions you could ask in this situation include "What is it about Uncle Tom you don't like?" or "What kind of 'bad things' does this boy do?"

Helpers need to recognize hidden signals an abused person may send (See Chapters 5 and 6). Once you have been able to help the victim verbalize his or her questions, you may wish to respond with answers along the lines described in this chapter.

Here are some examples of questions for which the victim of abuse may want answers. The exact way the questions would be answered would vary according to the age of the person wanting help.

Will you help me?

Willingness to help a victim of abuse needs to be clearly communicated in a positive way. Since an abused person usually has poor self-perception, he or she may interpret hesitancy by the helper as personal rejection. When a helper anticipates involvement in this type of situation, it is necessary to know what he or she is being asked to do and what may be involved. It is also important to know as much as possible about the situation.

Because involvement in cases of abuse can be demanding, the helper must be aware of his or her own resources and energy and be familiar with the network of caring people who work together within the Church. In the past I have overestimated my own ability and, consequently, volunteered more than my existing resources and energy. I am learning to be realistic in the amount of help I can promise. Here are some of the ways I am able to help victims of abuse:

- Write your thoughts out on paper, and I will read anything you mail to me.
- If it would be a benefit to you and to our family, you may live with us for three months.
- Phone me once a week. We can talk for about an hour.

There are many other ways help can be given to abuse victims:

- Provide housing for a family when domestic violence threatens.
- Advise a parent on child rearing.
- Establish a hot-line intervention service.
- Become substitute grandparents.
- Invite the abused to go on vacations.
- Teach remedial skills.
- Offer big-brother relationships.
- Establish after-school child care.
- Find jobs for single parents.
- Extend invitations to extended family gatherings, especially at the holiday season.

A helper can say to the victim of abuse, "Yes, I will help. I can support you as you begin the journey toward emotional health. I can guide you to people who have expertise—people who are trained in the area of your need."

The best help that can be given a victim of abuse is the gift of your time—time to listen with patience and without interruption, time to ask questions that help your understanding and encourage further revelation, time to learn what the person endured, time to communicate compassion by your presence. Giving a person your time can enhance the potential for self-healing within each abuse victim. Someone has said that we can listen a soul into being. Helpers need to give their time in this way.

When done in the name of Christ, things we do that may seem insignificant to us can make positive changes in the lives of those wounded by abuse. Many women wrote letters of thanks after Chapel of the Air broadcasted my series on abuse, stating "You give me hope" or "At last, someone recognizes abuse is a problem within the Church" or "Your words have given me courage to take action." I had done little for the hundreds of individuals reached by the broadcasts, but that little made significant impact on many lives.

If I tell you what happened to me, will you believe me?

This is another question to which it is very important to respond in a positive, reassuring way. But at times it can be very difficult to convey confidence in what the victim is telling you. This may especially be true if the victim of abuse reveals that the abuser is a person you know and respect.

This moment of revelation is crucial. The way in which the victim's story is received by the person he or she tells can make an enormous difference in working through what has happened. A negative, doubting response or reaction may compound the emotional damage already done, expose the victim to further abuse, and destroy communication between you and the victim. If the accuracy and reliability of the victims story is questioned, it will likely be a long time, if ever, before he or she will risk revealing the painful events again.

It is important not to overreact or become enraged at the incidents that are being told. The abused person is already coping with his or her own emotions and should not have to respond to the helper's emotions as well. It is understandable, however, that the helper might respond with anger. Communicate to the victim that the anger is not directed at him or her but at the person who violated them.

We must learn to say to the victim, "Yes, I believe you. I believe that these terrible things happened to you. I believe that you are telling the truth. I want to hear what you have to say, and I want to help you."

One of the first women, who came from a background of incest with whom I worked, lived for a while in our home. Often, when she received a phone call from her family, she became so terrified that she experienced an extreme physiological reaction. Her hands and feet would perspire so profusely that they would drip.

Memories of incest were just beginning to surface in her mind. Her young husband said to me, "Do you believe what my wife is saying really happened to her? Or is this psychosis?"

Fortunately, I did believe, though I understood little about her pain or the psychodynamics of intrafamily sexual abuse. I told him that I thought these things had happened to her because she had such an intense physical reaction. (I was beginning to learn that cause is in proportion to effect.) Anyone whose hands and feet drip perspiration because of a telephone conversation has some cause for that reaction.

Having heard many sordid stories of abuse has alleviated any tendency I might have to disbelieve. Nowadays, I find myself responding in compassion. The most merciful action I know is to listen fully and believingly to everything the victim needs to tell me.

If I tell you what happened to me, will you promise not to tell anyone?

It would not be wise to promise that no one else will ever be told information that you hear concerning cases of abuse. But it is possible to assure an abuse victim that only people who are needed to help him or her would be told what has happened. It may also be necessary to talk to someone who can try to help the perpetrator of the abuse.

Victims of intrafamily abuse want the injustice to stop. But, at the same time, they are often emotionally dependent on the abuser. This is especially true in incestuous families. A victim of incest may have a bittersweet relationship with the abuser. On one hand, there may be anger and fear toward the abuser due to emotional and physical pain inflicted; but on the other hand, the victim may crave the attention and affection of the abuser. The physical affection shown the victim both creates and fills a need. A victim of incest may also fear that if the situation is revealed to anyone, the family will break up or the father will be put in jail.

Efforts need to be made to prevent further abuse from occurring. Steps necessary to do this would vary with each situation, but abuse rarely stops without intervention. The abuser usually needs to be removed from the home for a time. This sounds like a difficult, drastic step, but the welfare of all involved must be kept in mind. It is necessary to take action that insures the violator will not commit the abusive acts against another person.

In most situations the abuse victim needs to be assured that the violator will be cared for.

The things that happened to me were awful. Should I try to forget them and not talk about them?
Experts are of the opinion that it is necessary for the victim to try to recall incidents of abuse and tell them to an understanding listener. This is often the first step in healing the pain of the atrocities committed against him or her.

Encourage the victim to go to someone she trusts to discuss these things. The person may choose to talk to you. Be careful to wait until the person is ready to talk; don't try to rush this process by thinking that, if she just hurries up and gets it all out, she can start healing. It is essential that the time be right for disclosing the past, and no one but the victim can know when that time is.

Am I the only one this has happened to?
The relief of knowing others have suffered in similar ways seems to make the burden of abuse more bearable. The victim needs to know that these kinds of things have happened to other children and adults. One woman wrote, "When my sisters and I were growing up, sexually abused by our stepfather, we didn't realize that we were a few statistical points in a large and growing population. . . ."

For many victims of abuse, the healing process accelerates when they research literature on the subject, listen to the media bring public attention to this hidden darkness, and join a therapy group. It is comforting for them to hear "This is what happened to me" and then be able to share their own story as a response.

The isolation and secrecy of abuse is one of the agonies of this problem. We must say to the battered wife, the victim of child abuse, and to the sexually violated child (or adult revealing a past incident), "No, you are not the only one. This has happened to others."

41

I'm ugly. I feel dirty. I'm no good to anyone. What's wrong with me?

A victim of abuse is likely to ask this question. His or her self-perception is usually distorted by the awful things that have been done. Abused people may need assistance realizing that they are special and worthy of being helped. The abused may perceive themselves as having little value or usefulness.

However, abused children are not likely to ask this question, because, prior to adolescence, children are not able to express how they think others perceive them. It is possible to detect poor self-esteem in children by watching them relate to others, enter activities, and conduct themselves, but rarely will they be able to tell you how they feel.

Regardless of age or verbalizing this question, an abused person desperately needs to be told that he or she is valuable, full of potential, attractive—not ugly or dirty—and able to be loved.

I saw this negative self-image in a woman I had been trying to help for months. After one particularly harried time together, the woman asked, "Do you still love me?" When I replied that, indeed, I did, she said, "That's incredible!" She was truly amazed that I thought her worthy of my love.

My husband David is wonderful about saying words of love to people who need to hear them. He doesn't just think them or tell me after the person has left. I've watched him, time and again, put his arm around someone, give them a brotherly hug, and say, "You are something else! How in the world have you managed to become what you are! You are a beautiful woman, and you've done remarkable things in your life!"

The victim needs to hear encouraging words. One survivor of abuse asked me what she looked like. Her self-image was so damaged that she wasn't sure she was accurately seeing herself in a mirror. We need to tell these people that we value who they are and what we sense they can become.

We can help elevate a people's self-esteem by accepting them, making them feel cared for, and including them in our lives. We want them to feel that they belong. We also want to help them realize they can do important and worthwhile things so that they feel competent.

The rest of these questions would usually be asked by adult victims rather than children.

Am I losing my mind?

The victim of abuse has experienced emotionally and psychologically painful things. It can be very disturbing when memories of these events invade his or her thoughts. Talking about these thoughts is very helpful—in fact, it may be essential—for healing.

Because unbelievable acts have been imposed upon the victims of abuse, they may react to the past with emotional, psychological, and physical responses which may seem irrational. A great fear of insanity sometimes develops among the survivors of abuse. Surfacing memories of past acts may also be met with disbelief on the part of victims which can make it difficult for them to cope. They react, "This can't have happened to me! I must be going crazy."

Do I need professional help?

When a person has been dealing with an issue for a long time and doesn't know how to make progress or get help from family or friends, he or she would probably benefit from professional counsel.

It is not always easy to know if the best counsel for the individual would be from a ministry professional or a mental health professional. Often a fine line exists between which type of help would be best. Sometimes a difficult situation can arise. A friend had to admit his wife to the psychiatric ward of a health center after well-meaning Christians attempted to exorcise demons from her. What she really had needed was mental health care.

M. Scott Peck, the best-selling author of *The Road Less Traveled*, in a lecture stated a rule of thumb for knowing when professional care is needed is—when stuck, get help. In his book Peck wrote that deciding to seek counseling or psychotherapy is one of the hardest, yet most courageous and significant decisions an individual can make.

Valuable help may be found through a variety of means:
- a spiritual mentor who understands the victim's background of abuse.
- sympathetic, caring friends who can listen.
- a relationship with another abuse survivor to help each other grow.
- professional counseling.

Why did God allow this to happen to me? Where was God when I needed Him?

When a person asks "why" questions about God, he or she may sometimes receive an answer right away. But usually a long wait is needed before one learns why God allowed difficult things to come into his or her life. God knows how hard and painful these situations are. But He has promised in His Word that everything that comes into the lives of those who love and belong to Him will work, in time, for good (Rom. 8:28).

God understands how angry and confused we feel about unjust things that happen to us. He is able to absorb the impact of these emotions because He is the One who has borne our sorrows. In time He allows us to feel the pulse of His broken heart, because He suffers when we suffer.

Can I ever be a whole, normal, functioning person?

The victim of abuse needs to be shown Scripture that promises, through Christ's redemptive work, anyone can be set free from an old life. The confidence that this can happen is based on two truths—first, God is powerful; second, other survivors of abuse have found wholeness in Christ. The guarantee has been given that the indwelling Holy Spirit will comfort in moments of bitter agony and perform the emotional and psychological surgery that is needed to bring about wholeness.

By coming to terms with Scriptural truth, receiving love and support from the Christian community, and having courage to take the psychological journey required for healing, the abused can be set free from the scars of abuse and experience wholeness. Wholeness is really maturity, and each of us develops it in different ways.

How long does it take for the pain to go away?

The healing process differs from person to person. For some, it can seem instantaneous; but for most people, the process is slow, tedious, and deliberate.

Psychological healing is comparable to physical healing. While a scratch or a sprained ankle heals relatively quickly, multiple injuries caused by a terrible accident may take months, if not years, to mend. The impact of the accident may have shattered bones and torn internal organs. First must come delicate surgery to repair the damage. Then comes a long period of recovery. The wounds inflicted by the accident and the surgeon's scalpel must both heal. So it is with the pain of abusive incidents and the pain of disclosing them. Growth and healing always seem to be accompanied by pain.

We all want to be free of pain. We don't enjoy the slow, deliberate rehabilitation process that brings about healing. We would prefer instant cures. Expecting quick healing from the traumas of abuse is as simplistic as saying, "Why do I have to have this tumor removed? Won't it just go away?"

Sometimes it is necessary to ask a question of the abuse victim. One such question would be: "Do you want to be healed?"

This is the same question Christ asked of the man by the pool of Bethsaida. He had been ill for 38 years and was waiting for an angel to trouble the waters so he could enter them and be healed. But why had he waited so long?

This question should be asked of the person who wonders if he or she can ever lead a normal life—without emotional disorders, irrational compulsions, physical upsets, and relational failures. The person, who has struggled with the past for a long time, may need to be asked "Do you want to get well? Do you really want to be whole? If so, are you willing to do anything to allow God freedom to make you whole—even to 'take up your pallet and walk'?" Without a doubt, God is the divine Therapist who oversees rehabilitation of every victim, whose hand is nearby to squeeze when the pain becomes intense, and who makes sure, if trust is placed in Him, that he or she can rest secure. But God also insists that, if wholeness is desired, the responsibility for the work must be shared.

Wholeness is a joint venture between the human and the Divine. Many are still not whole because they have expected God to do it all; and many are still not whole because they have attempted to do it all by themselves.

Yes, we can say to the victims of abuse, "You can be whole, but it is going to take deliberate work and a firm hold on the belief that God is able to bring wholeness to your life."

Chapter 4

Counseling the Abused

To *counsel* means to establish a special kind of relationship with a person—a relationship in which the counselor uses special skills to help resolve a problem the other person has. In order to provide counsel, the helper must be accessible and communicate a willingness to enter into this kind of relationship. Counsel may be provided in an informal setting—in a kitchen over a cup of coffee; or it can be formal—in an office at a prearranged time.

Counseling, in its simplest form, can take place when a person *listens* to what another needs to share. Emotional healing can begin when a troubled person is able to share a problem with a compassionate listener. Merely explaining the dilemma often can help bring resolution.

In this chapter we want to go beyond this beginning level of counsel and examine additional means for helping another to resolve problems.

Basics About Counseling

Many people who are professionally involved in ministry have had training in basic counseling skills. But a tremendous amount of work for God's Kingdom is done by His people who never have had courses or even seminars in counseling.

In any counseling situation, the helper must be careful not to promise more than he or she is able to accomplish. Often it is necessary to say something like "I can do _____ for you, but I cannot do _____." This indicates that the complexities of the problem are recognized, as well as the personal energies and resources of the helper. This also requires delineating between the help that can be provided by networking within the church community and by professionals who specialize in mental health. It is essential that the counselor make his or her limitations clear.

People who minister to others need to keep in mind a basic framework for structuring counseling situations. William R.

Miller and Kathleen A. Jackson have written *Practical Psychology for Pastors* (Prentice-Hall, 1985) which contains this kind of help. They suggest that the following four questions be used as guides for an approach to working with people who may have a variety of problems—not just abuse:

1. *What is the nature of the problem?*

Problems affect people in a variety of ways. To determine if *emotions* or feelings may be involved, ask questions about how the person feels right now and if that is different from how he or she has felt in the past. There may be *behavior patterns* which affect the situation. It can be helpful to ask questions like "What do you do when . . ." or "What happens if . . ." Finally, the problem may be affected by the person's *thoughts* or perceptions of his or her world. To determine this, questions can be asked that will help the person talk about what he or she believes or thinks.

Sometimes the problem is obvious and can be determined easily by watching and listening to the person. Other times, there may be conflict between what the person claims is the problem and how it appears to you. For example, a mother could come to you for help in how to handle a delinquent, rebellious child. The child might appear to be the problem, but sensitive questioning could reveal that neglect or abuse of the child by one of the parents is the real problem. This is why focusing questions on those three areas—emotions, behavior, and feelings—can help you and the person understand what is going on. Many times underlying relational conflicts will be revealed.

2. *What is the cause of the problem?*

Rarely is the answer to this question obvious. Most problems do not have simple solutions because they do not have simple causes. There are usually many causes to a problem. Miller and Jackson state that there are four types of causes:

- A *primary cause* is one which must be present for the problem to exist or one which is sufficient to cause a problem for anyone.
- A *predisposing cause* is a factor that leaves the person susceptible to the problem.
- A *precipitating cause* is something that happens immediately before the problem develops (often the greater, underlying

cause is overlooked because of the attention demanded by this immediate problem).

• A *perpetuating cause* is one that allows the problem to continue.

Given these four types of causes, it is interesting to go back and analyze the case studies in Chapter 3 of this book in light of this information.

3. *What is missing from the person's life?*

When considering this question, the counselor needs to get an overview of the person's life. To determine what is missing from a person's life is not an easy task and often requires intuition on the part of the counselor.

The three most important aspects on which to focus are the person's view of self, relationships, and work or productivity. These areas have great importance in emotional and psychological health. Finding lack of fulfillment in one of these can be significant. Each of us, even a young schoolchild, needs to feel good about himself or herself, to be cared for by someone, and to feel he or she does some kind of work well. Then the counselor should help to determine what can be done to fill the deficiencies in the person's life.

4. *What does the person need?*

A major part of counseling is to help the person determine what needs to be done. It is not the job of the counselor to do what is needed but to present options and possible consequences of those options. The action that is usually needed is to make some kind of change, reach a decision on an issue, or reduce areas of life that are confusing or chaotic.

An important service that a lay counselor can perform is to help the person realize the need for professional help and act on that realization. Following the guideline "if you don't know what to do, get help," the lay counselor will often need to refer a person to someone with more expertise. But this can be difficult and confusing because there are so many types of mental health professionals. Here are some basic explanations of who does what in psychosocial therapy:

Psychiatrist—A physician who has additional specialized training in mental health disorders. These therapists may prescribe medications and perform treatments.

Psychologist—A person who specialized in the study of the mind and behavior. A clinical psychologist has a doctor of philosophy degree qualifying him or her to evaluate and treat mental and emotional problems.

Psychiatric social worker—A counselor with a master's degree in social work. This person's focus is on helping an individual adjust within the community.

Marriage and/or Family counselor—A person with at least a master's level of training who specializes in the problems and dynamics of relationships within marriage and the family.

Pastoral Counselor—A member of the clergy who focuses on providing spiritual direction, pastoral guidance, and interpretation of Scripture. Although there are no established criteria, these people have usually obtained advanced psychological training.

Counseling the Battered Wife

A woman who is beaten by her husband may sometimes have difficulty finding a sympathetic listener. This may be because her husband behaves differently in public than he does privately. "To believe" her means that something must be done to help her. It means becoming embroiled in the problems of a malfunctioning marriage.

The *Time* magazine issue on abuse (September 5, 1983) stated that the reason for this disbelief is rooted in an attitude that says, "There is nothing new about wife beating. Often it is accepted as a natural if regrettable part of woman's status as her husband's property." All too often, misinterpretation of Scripture relating to husband/wife roles encourages this attitude of domination. At its worst this mistaken theology supplies the abuser with an excuse for active violence against his wife.

The Rev. Paul Simmons (see the first case study in Chapter 3), after his experience of trying to counsel Donna Anderson, began to research Christian literature on the topic of wife battering. In *No Place to Hide* by Esther Lee Olson with Kenneth Peterson (Tyndale House, 1982), he found a list of ten steps an abused wife should take to protect herself. These are guidelines which Simmons wished he had known when Donna Anderson came to him for help. They are also good aids for any Christian helper or minister who is working with a victim of domestic violence. Giving a woman these guidelines and helping her carry them out is a powerful way of saying "I believe you." The victim needs to know that the following steps are ways to break out of the prison in which she finds herself.

1. *Pray.* For the Christian this is the easy one to say, the obvious one to hear, and the important step that is rarely used or used in the wrong way.

2. *If your life is threatened, leave the home.*

3. *Let others know about the problem.* The idea here is to create a network of aware people (pastor, doctor, parents, close friends) who will not suddenly be surprised when an incident erupts. They should be ready to establish support systems when needed.

4. *Communicate your anger to your husband.* The best way to do this is in the presence of a third party who will help the communication process. This should not be at a time when explosive emotions are present.

5. *Determine what it would take to cause you to leave your husband. Plan ahead so you'll be prepared if that day comes.*

6. *If physical abuse occurs three times, leave the home.* [The authors of the book (Olson and Peterson) feel that] three abusive attacks constitute a pattern. Intervention is definitely indicated to prevent future occurrences.

7. *Make sure the new living accommodations are safe from the abuser.*

8. *See your physician.* This verifies that violence has occurred and provides immediate medical treatment and attention for obvious and internal injuries.

9. *Seek a supportive community of people.* If there ever was a time a woman needed warm, sympathetic, caring friends, it is now. Possible resources to explore are a domestic violence hot line, a support group for battered women, the director of women's ministries at a local church, or a pastor's wife who knows how to relate to people in pain.

10. *Find a counselor.* The damage from abuse is often extensive and long-lasting. Don't attempt to continue in the marriage without some professional marital counseling and intervention.

Severe mercy needs to be shown to the battering male to protect the lives of the wife and children. Deterrences need to be established for a man who has established physical abuse as a behavioral pattern. Many of these men rationalize their behavior outrageously. As a result they need to be coerced and pressured by outside forces to face the truth of their actions.

A supportive relationship needs to be maintained with an abuse victim even while he or she is receiving professional help. During this counsel painful memories can be exposed or difficult steps to resolve the problem may be suggested. The survivor of abuse needs help in working through these things.

One woman to whom I recommended professional counseling calls me after particularly traumatic therapy sessions. A psychologist with whom I consult warned me about allowing myself to become *triangulated*, a situation in which the counselee pits an outside opinion against the recommendations of the therapist. With that advice in mind, I nevertheless cautiously concluded that this woman really did need to debrief the perplexing, confusing, and overwhelming truths she was beginning to realize. Talking things over with me, being able to say, "What do you think about this? Is that okay? He said that I . . ." was all part of the process of integrating this psychological journey with the rest of her personality.

Counseling the Abused Child

The teacher, youth worker, or neighbor is the one who most frequently becomes aware of evidence of child abuse by watching the way the child acts. A child's behavior is often a symptom of the neglect that is occurring in his home. He or she will unintentionally act out the hidden deprivations and abuses that are being experienced.

It is difficult for those who have not come from a background of abuse to understand the utter degradation, the feelings of worthlessness and self-hatred, and the loss of motivation that many victims experience. A child who has been verbally denigrated every day has few tender moments in his or her memory bank. This child learns to mistrust tenderness because "tenderness" can too easily become an enraged slap, kick, shove, or punch.

My husband and I have found this to be true during our ministry to youth. Not long ago we received a phone call from a woman who had been in a Bible club when we worked with Youth for Christ. I barely remembered this teen from 25 years ago, but my husband had better recall and warmly greeted her over the phone. "I just wanted to tell you," said the voice on the other end of the line, "I've just received my master's degree in psychology, and I thought back over the people who have made a significant difference in my life. You couldn't possibly have known it at the time, but my father abused me in every way, emotionally, sexually, physically. Somehow, by the grace of

God, I have survived and am becoming a healthy adult. But when I think back on those teen years when I felt so filthy, so self-hating, it was your love, and the times you had me into your home, and the way you believed in me that helped me make it through adolescence. I just wanted to call and make sure I said thanks."

The love of a concerned adult *can* make all the difference in an abused child's life. We were just "there" for this young woman; we didn't engage in any lengthy counseling regime, but we showed that we cared about her and told her of God's love.

Guidelines for referring children for professional help are more difficult to set than for adults. David A. Kahn, M.D., Assistant Professor of Child Psychiatry at Hahnemann Medical College in Philadelphia, doesn't think therapy is necessarily indicated for most children. Short-term symptoms of the abuse incident are expected. There may be nightmares, fears, tears, bed-wetting, etc. If these symptoms persist beyond a few months, the child may benefit from professional help. But it is the parents, he thinks, who may benefit most by discussing their responses and emotions with a trusted counselor. It is the parent who conveys security to the child, who explains, interprets, and protects. Parents who are confident in their roles will give confidence to their children. This is why helping the parents of abused kids is the best way to help the kids.

A child protection assessment worker in Dakota County, Minnesota, gave this advice at a workshop I attended:

If you as a neighbor, friend, or relative hear a child, however obliquely, refer to his or her parent as abusive, listen carefully to what is being said and attempt to ask sensitive questions that will not frighten the child. It's important not to promise the child that action will be taken to stop the abuse. Broken promises are something that the child may be all too accustomed to. Rather, you might reassure the child that you care, that you will continue to listen, and would like to ask the help of someone accustomed to handling such problems.

Counseling Victims of Incest

In order to help the victim of incest, it is necessary to understand the dynamics of the relationships and emotions involved. The victim of incest may be a child, an adolescent, or an adult who is coming to terms with sexual abuse he or she experienced

53

as a child. Many have coped with the trauma of abuse by hiding the act or acts so completely that the knowledge of this pain has been completely buried psychologically.

The tragedy of incest may have provided the victim with the most intimate sharing experiences the victim knows. If the acts are presently occurring, disclosure means disruption of the incidents and removal and punishment of the perpetrator. If the incest is in the past, disclosure means violating an internal emotional structure the victim has erected in order to be able to cope with why this has happened.

Noreen is an example of a person who erected coping structures, but they were very negative ones. She had undergone psychiatric care throughout college due to the effects of a long-term incestuous relationship that had taken place from childhood through adolescence, but she never told anyone, even her therapist, about the sexual abuse. A few years later Noreen became suicidal. She considered driving herself and her children off a cliff. She was plagued by mood swings. Finally, in desperation, she shoplifted, thinking the courts would assign her to someone who would help her. To her dismay, she was jailed, fined, and released without anyone ever asking why she had committed the crime.

The victim of incest often takes upon himself or herself the guilt of the perpetrator. Experts in the field stress that it is important for helpers to alleviate this mistaken sense of responsibility. Long-term, incestuous relationships can be compared to an adult injecting an addicting drug into the victim's bloodstream. A physical dependency develops because early exposure to sexual activity often creates sexual cravings difficult for a child or adolescent to control. This young victim becomes caught in a relationship of sexual and emotional bondage with the violator—much like the addict with the drug dealer. But this victim is not responsible for the entrapment. The guilt belongs to the perpetrator of the act. The victim of incest has to deal with the effects of the "habit," not the guilt of the violation. He or she is a victim. A victim is someone upon whom unrighteousness has been imposed.

David B. Peters in *A Betrayal of Innocence: What Everyone Should Know About Child Sexual Abuse* (Word Books, 1986) lists ways to respond to a child who needs to tell someone that he or she has been sexually abused. Although these guidelines are written to the parent of a sexually abused child, the principles are important for any who wants to help such a child.

1. Take your child to a private place and ask your child to explain in his or her own words. Listen carefully and remember to be calm and matter-of-fact.
2. Believe your child! Children seldom lie about sexual abuse.
3. Assure your child that what happened is not his or her fault, and that you are glad you have been told.
4. Tell your child you are sorry he or she was hurt and frightened and that you will protect him or her from further abuse.
5. Call an agency that has expertise in the field of sexual abuse. Most areas have a child protective service agency. Check with local law enforcement agencies for information.
6. If what your child says causes you to suspect that sexual penetration or physical injury has occurred, seek medical attention for your child immediately, and inform the doctor of your suspicions.
7. Take whatever steps are necessary to protect your child from further abuse. In the case of incest, see that the molester, not the victim, leaves the home.

Later in the book, Peters provides several factors that help determine the degree of potential emotional damage done to the victim of incest.

1. *The relationship of the molester to the victim:* The more closely related or highly trusted the molester, the more damage done to the child.
2. *The use of violence:* The more force or violence, the greater the damage, especially if serious physical injuries result.
3. *The degree of nonviolent coercion:* The greater the amount of fear and guilt used in controlling the victim, the more serious the damage.
4. *The extent of abuse:* Intercourse is more emotionally harmful than genital exposure or other noncontact forms of abuse. However, excessive and long-term fondling has been found in some instances to rival the damage caused by intercourse.
5. *The duration of abuse:* Sexual abuse which takes place over a long period of time tends to be more harmful than that of short duration.
6. *The number and frequency of incidents:* The more numerous and frequent the incidents, the greater the emotional damage.
7. *The reactions of significant adults to the report of abuse:* The less emotional support the victim receives from family members and the community, the greater the degree of damage.

Researchers agree that the moment when a child reveals incestuous activity to a mother (or any other person) is crucial: *the mother's support and belief in a child's revelation of incest are the most important elements in a child's recovery.* A second important ingredient in that healing process is the perpetrator's assumption of guilt and taking the blame upon himself. This should be sought if at all possible.

From my experiences counseling victims of incest, there are three critical phases in the life of a sexual abuse survivor when special help may be needed. It is wise to be aware of these times and to provide special assistance if needed. These are (a) immediately after the abuse occurs, (b) at the time of the victim's marriage, and (c) when the victim's children are the age when she experienced the abuse.

The victims of childhood sexual abuse are not only victims, but also survivors; and despite their strange reactions and puzzling behavior, they need to be affirmed for the tenacious way they have clung to life and sanity and have struggled toward normalcy. Many survivors of incest testify to the fact that recovery and a normal life are possible.

The families of incest victims need special consideration. Tamar Cohen wrote an article titled "The Incestuous Family Revisited" in *Social Casework: The Journal of Contemporary Social Work* (March, 1983). She states, "The dynamics of the classic incestuous family indicate that all the family members are emotionally deprived, that the sexually taboo relationship is a manifestation of basic need for warmth and nurturance, and that its continuation provides a defense against possible family break-up." Awareness of the complexity of the problem may prevent a helper from volunteering to take on a needy family system.

A closer look at the mother of the victim provides a clearer picture of the dynamics of an incestuous triangle. This woman sometimes fits the textbook picture of a *passive-collusive* personality. Maxine Hancock and I wrote this in our book *Child Sexual Abuse: A Hope for Healing*:

The mother who has discovered that the abuser is her own husband, or the child's father or stepfather, finds her role excruciatingly complicated. There is a triad that demands resolution—her child, the victim; her husband, the betrayer; herself, the betrayed—not to mention the rest of her family. . . .

Second only to the victim herself, the mother of the victim suffers the most profound emotional upheaval. Her immediate reaction is one of shock. She may feel a gamut of emotions in rapid succession—

repulsion so strong that it ventures on actual physical nausea; confusion as she is torn between a whirlwind of polar loyalties (to her child, to her husband whom she still loves); jealousy which is soon supplanted by a deep, bedrock conviction of failure; betrayal by both her husband and daughter. . . .

And the mother experiences grief at the loss of her marital relationship—how can it ever be the same? How can she ever trust her husband again? Her security is shattered as well as her hopes for the future. She is also faced with possible financial uncertainty if he is arrested or the marriage is dissolved.

No woman under any other stress—death, severe illness—needs more support.

In some situations, the mother is maladjusted—all too often a victim of abuse or incest herself. In many incestuous families, she has become passive and allows things to happen that she feels are too big for her to handle. In these situations, mother/daughter role reversal may develop. The mother may become dependent upon the child, or she may be absent because of work, emotional unresponsiveness, or illness. When this happens, the daughter begins to function as a surrogate wife—a child/mother to the mother/child.

In one study incest survivors, examined many years later, indicated that anger at the mother was a serious problem in adult life. Of the daughters studied, 40 percent continued to experience strong negative feelings toward their fathers, while the others could be described as forgiving though resentful from time to time. The opposite results were found with regard to the mothers—60 percent were disliked by their daughters, while 40 percent were regarded more positively.

An increasing number of observers, however, are beginning to find fault with the concept of the mother as a causative factor in incest. Sometimes maternal negligence is involved; other times there is a passivity that amounts to collusion; but in a great number of cases this is not so. The mother is truly a victim as well.

The Nanaimo Rape/Assault Center lists several helps for these mothers in its manual *Realities of Child Sexual Abuse*:

1. The mother of an incest victim, especially at the time of disclosure, is suffering a major life trauma and will need massive support.
2. The mother may have requested help in the past and may need assistance in counteracting negative messages of blame or disbelief.

3. The mother's need for support, reinforcement, and acceptance will continue for a lengthy period as she strives to deal with the emotional damage done to her and her child.

4. The mother may require assistance with such everyday concerns as food and housing for herself and her children.

5. The mother may find herself in interaction with the legal, criminal justice, and human resources systems. She may need information about their procedures and emotional support when dealing with them.

6. The mother's traditional support systems may be disrupted as friends and family react in various ways to her situation. She may be under intense pressure from these people to refrain from taking any action against the offender. She may need support in the decisions she makes, whatever they may be.

7. The mother may fear for her emotional stability, as she undergoes the usual responses to her disrupted life. She needs reassurance that her reactions are expected and manageable.

8. The mother needs constant reiteration of these messages: "I believe you." "You are not the offender." "Your emotions are acceptable." "You and your child can recover."

For more information regarding the work of this center, write:
Nanaimo Rape/Assault Center
105-285 Prideaux Street
Nanaimo, British Columbia V9R 2N2

Providing Spiritual Counsel

One of the most important things a Christian helper can provide for a survivor of abuse is spiritual counsel. Each of us can be ministers of spiritual and relational reconciliation for those who have endured personal injustice. Here is a model for spiritual counsel that I have used when helping women heal from the trauma of childhood incest. This model may be adapted for providing spiritual counsel to the victim of any type of abuse.

Kathy (not her real name) revealed that an older uncle enticed her into a long-term incestuous relationship beginning when she was five and continuing for almost seven years. It ended when one of them moved away. He was 19 when the abuse started. Intercourse occurred as often as twice a week. She writes, "All of this developed gradually. He started taking me to the barn to be alone with him. Later, he began to fondle me and expose himself to me, and ask me to kiss and handle him. I knew within myself that this wasn't right, but he kept telling me that this was our secret and that I wasn't ever to tell anybody. He promised he would never hurt me."

If Kathy came to you with the story of her past, how would you help her?

You may be a pastor, lay worker, teacher of the adult Sunday school class; you may be involved in the women's ministries of your church; or you may simply be a Christian friend. This woman has chosen to reveal to you the burden of a past which is damaging her development and growth as an adult.

You are inexperienced in helping victims of abuse, and you have little knowledge of the problem. The truth is, even without psychological expertise, you can do a great deal for Kathy.

The first time I heard from Kathy was by letter. She had attended a woman's conference where I had spoken on forgiveness. I had led the group in private prayers of confession for the sins they had committed and forgiveness toward those who had sinned against them.

Kathy, a registered nurse, had been under psychiatric care because of a suicide attempt during nursing school. But she never had revealed her past. Now she was married, had children, and was struggling with depression, suicidal tendencies, uncontrollable impulses, flashbacks of awful memories, and personality disorders. No one was aware that for years she had been an incest victim.

People who have endured the crime of incest often do not reveal the incidents unless they are specifically asked. One incest survivor expressed, "We talked about all kinds of family problems but [the therapist] never asked me about the big one—incest. You see, I had this kind of magical thing—if someone would say the word, I'd talk about it, but I couldn't bring the subject up. If I did, and my dad went to jail, it would be my fault. But, if someone else brought it up, it would be their fault!" The taboos that surround abuse have a strong negative hold on many of its victims.

Though Kathy was not yet a Christian, she was searching for meaning and purpose for her life. She had been attending a women's Bible study because it provided some time away from her children. Here, one of the women invited her to the retreat.

As I described in my message the condition of a woman's soul after living in a world filled with sin, Kathy realized that I was describing her. When I asked the group to confess their own sins and ask God's forgiveness for those sins, Kathy did so. But when I asked the group to begin forgiving the ones who had wounded them, Kathy thought, "She can't mean this. She can't be asking me to forgive my uncle." At that point, Kathy realized what she was saying. She had just asked God to forgive her and had sensed His forgiveness, but now she wasn't willing to offer her uncle what she had just received.

Reluctantly, with clenched fists, gritting her teeth, she realized she needed emotional healing too much to hold on to her resentment. She prayed, "*O.K., Lord, I'm willing to forgive him.*"

Kathy testifies that this difficult moment was a turning point in her journey toward wholeness. She went home and told her husband, "My life's never going to be the same from this day on. I don't know what has happened, and I can't explain it yet, but I'm sure things are going to be different." The inward change became obvious. In time Kathy's husband said to their children, "I don't know what's happened to Mommy—but we have a new mommy in this house."

Kathy's journey to wholeness, which provides a complete case study by Maxine Hancock and myself in our book *Child Sexual Abuse* can be a model for the Christian worker who feels too inadequate and inexperienced to be able to help. Kathy had been severely abused as a child because of a prolonged incestuous relationship. She was manifesting adult personality distress proportionate to the severity of the injustice. Although her journey has been long and difficult, she has become emotionally stable because of her commitment to the essential, but painful, growth process. Although this would not be recommended for most situations, during this journey toward spiritual wholeness, Kathy never underwent professional therapy.

1. THE NEED FOR FORGIVENESS

What took place in her life that made this journey so successful? This journey began with Kathy receiving God's forgiveness for sins she committed because of the perverted acts done to her.

Revelation or disclosure is confession. When an incest victim discloses to someone his or her sexual abuse, it may be the first attempt to confess, or it may be one of many attempts. In either case, the victim is extremely anxious and concerned about the listener's reaction. This is a crucial moment.

Alice Huskey, director of Counter Abuse, Inc., a group which specializes in training churches to work with the abused, wrote an article for *Youthworker* magazine (Winter, 1985). She says, "Remember too that the primary spiritual issue is the victim's need to forgive the abuser, for this opens the way for God's healing ministry in individual lives." Forgiveness is the essential activity which must be experienced if the trauma of the past is to be healed. Forgiveness must occur before significant emotional or psychological progress can take place.

When a woman comes to me with a story that sickens my soul, I give her the gift of listening. I choose to believe what she is telling me, no matter how incredible it seems, because she has a need to tell me those things. At some time, I will ask gently, "Have you received God's forgiveness for those areas in your life where you bear true guilt? Have you ever forgiven the person—the parent, the stranger, the friend, the relative—who did this to you?"

It is necessary to help abuse victims distinguish between the acts initiated against them and their responses to those acts. They are not guilty because of the evil brought on them, but they are responsible for the sins they committed because of their reaction to the abuse. Some of these sins are self-abuse, unrighteous anger, unjustified anger against innocent acquaintances, bitterness, vengefulness, becoming an abuser themselves, breaking God's commandments, hatefulness, and self-pity.

The act of forgiveness cannot be forced upon them, but Scriptures that teach forgiveness and promise cleansing can be explained. These victims need to realize that this cleansing occurs when we confess our own sins to God *and* when we forgive those who have sinned against us. "Therefore confess your sins to one another . . . that you may be healed," James 5:16 (RSV). I ask them to tell me when they are ready to do this spiritual work, and I volunteer to listen to their confessions and words of forgiveness for those who have damaged, if not ruined their lives (a ruin which God can supernaturally restore).

The victim of abuse needs to know that forgiveness for our sins comes directly from God who takes the guilt from us. Then God wants to hear that we forgive those who have violated us. Something supernatural occurs when this is done—the pain of the past begins to ease; the memories begin to heal.

But because we are emotional beings, most of us need a

person to represent Christ as we take this spiritual step—someone to hold our hands, someone to see our tears, someone to listen to our words. When we speak words of forgiveness aloud and know we are heard by God, spiritual work is accomplished—*and we know it*.

Often, when helping an abuse victim work through this process, I ask her to write out her confession and prayer of forgiveness. When she is ready, I have her read these prayers to me. I pray with her and quote from I John 1:9 (RSV), "If [you] confess [your] sins, he is faithful and just and will forgive [your] sins and cleanse [you] from all unrighteousness." I speak the words of Christ, "My child, your sins are forgiven you." I ask her to record His words at the bottom of the paper on which she has written her confession but to substitute her name to personalize His pronouncement. Other Scriptures may also be helpful, such as, "Receive the Holy Spirit. If you forgive the sins of any, they are forgiven; if you retain the sins of any, they are retained" (John 20:22, 23, RSV).

During these moments, as I kneel with this friend who has endured so much, I place my hand on her shoulders, indicating my willingness to be a channel for God's healing power to enter her life, sort of an informal laying on of hands. As Kathy testified, this powerful, spiritual moment can be the beginning of a radical, dramatic transformation. (Caution must be exercised when this type of counsel is done by the opposite sex. Touch can be misinterpreted. This caution is especially true when helping the sexually abused.)

When counseling victims of incest, one is often faced with the irrefutable evidence of evil playing havoc in the lives of helpless victims. There is a dark mastermind which instigates unspeakable acts which only the Church, beneath the shadow of Christ's cross, can fully redeem. In a sense, the laying on of hands, anointing with oil, the Eucharist (or celebration of Communion) all have healing potential to represent Christ through tangible means to the victim who has survived the evil effects of incest. The Church must not neglect the rites of confession and pronouncement of forgiveness because of the sense of purification and release that can come to participants.

When speaking to large groups at retreats, I have come to say, "I can't counsel with you. There are too many of you present, and very frankly, I don't have the skills. But I can bring you to

Christ, and we can begin to do the spiritual work which the Church has always traditionally offered.''

In my mind, to minister to those in need is synonymous to representing Christ to those who are fainthearted, whose spiritual vision is dimmed, who are weary due to the weight of bearing their own sins and the sins of those who have violated them. To minister means to speak on Christ's behalf—to say His thoughts, to act on His behalf—to do His works and to love as He would love. This is spiritual authority that is rarely exercised to its full potential.

Kathy's experience with forgiveness did not end at the women's retreat. For all practical purposes, I was out of her life, but someone still needed to minister to her. Though the flashbacks she had been experiencing miraculously ceased immediately, Kathy realized there was further spiritual work that needed to be done. A woman had become Kathy's prayer partner, and Kathy asked if she would work through with her each memory of incest in therapeutic forgiveness. Though Kathy had forgiven her uncle, received God's forgiveness, and experienced release from the past, she soon realized she had never forgiven herself for the effects the past had on her. This gave the enemy of her soul opportunity to defeat her with constant self-accusations.

Five or six afternoons in prayer with her partner were required before Kathy could bring God's presence to her first memory of incest. Finally, the memories began to surface. With the recall of each incident, she asked Christ to forgive her for wrong feelings, and she asked God to forgive her uncle. Then, before God and a human witness, she would announce, "And I forgive myself." This was a traumatic, painful journey, but one which freed Kathy. Over and over she would pray. "God forgive him. God forgive me. On the basis of Your Word, I claim that You have faithfully and justly forgiven and cleansed me." Then on to the next incident. This is the therapeutic work of prayer, and it is a labor of love which many of us are equipped to undertake.

The promise of confidentiality is imperative in this work. You must not tell another—not your spouse, housemate, or a close friend. This priestly work is the privilege of believers, but it is bound by an ethic of confidentiality as stringent as if a vow had been taken before legal authorities. The person who comes to you in emotional pain must believe that you can keep her secrets and that your tongue will not betray the naked revelations of her soul. This is why the details of all the stories in this book have been altered—to preserve confidentiality.

I frequently refer people who need psychological treatment to a friend who is a therapist. This professional won't even tell me if they have called her, much less any details of the counseling relationship. The counselees may choose to tell me what transpires in the sessions, but my friend will never reveal anything to me. Those of us who are vocational ministers and lay workers must learn to do the same.

2. THE NEED FOR ACCOUNTABILITY

The Christian worker needs to hold the victim of abuse who wants to become whole accountable for growth. This is a mutually agreeable contract which the counselor and the counselee develop. The fact that Kathy's prayer partner met with her weekly was a type of accountability that kept Kathy working on therapeutic forgiveness until they both sensed its purposes were accomplished. Accountability can be done over the phone. A situation might go like this: "You asked me to check on Wednesday to see if you had memorized those Scripture verses. Well, here I am, calling you. Have you done what you agreed to do? If not, why?"

Holding the victim of abuse who wants to grow accountable can stimulate healing and spiritual maturing. A situation may require you to say, "You said you were going to write that letter to your father this week, and you asked me to make sure you had done so. Have you written yet? Would you like me to read the letter? Have you mailed it?"

Spouses can hold one another accountable, but I have found that an objective outsider is able to prod more effectively. I often invite someone I trust to hold me accountable for certain areas of productivity or growth. Loving (not harsh, manipulative, or coercive) accountability can be very helpful for the abuse sufferer.

We may need to say to a battered wife "Have you found legal counsel yet?" " Have you told your parents what you are coping with?" "Have you seen a doctor?" This helps her overcome fear and reluctance. Accountability is a loving, compassionate person seeing that we do what we need to do.

There are many ways accountability can be used while working with people in difficult situations. One counselor I know draws up a weekly contract with abuse victims that come to her. This contract helps them get through the week until the next session. A prayer pact could be made so that, when suicidal thoughts threaten, the victim of abuse would call his or her partner for prayer. Praying with people over the phone is an effective way of meeting their needs. I have asked people to call me when they felt they were losing control so we could quietly pray together.

3. THE NEED FOR SCRIPTURE

The mind and thoughts of the abuse victim can often feel like they have been steeped in degradation. Kathy again becomes a model for us by her diligent approach to Scripture. Realizing that her custom of watching several hours of soap operas every afternoon was unprofitable, she began to use that time to study God's Word. Though she had been a good student in school, studying the Bible was difficult for her. She started with an inductive study of Philippians and prayed her way through each question. Her confidence began to grow as she became more familiar with the Bible. Soon she began to study great Biblical themes like God's sovereignty, His nature, and His covenants with us.

In time, as Kathy saturated her mind with Scripture, she began to feel renewed. The past lost its tenacious hold on her mind and emotions. She gave the trauma of her childhood to a God whom she now really believed cared, ruled, ordained, and intervened. Not long ago Kathy wrote, ". . . I have seen the grace of God in a marvelous way. And God has taught me so much." This statement is evidence of a miracle of God's grace.

Scripture is a tool we must give the survivor of abuse. Psychiatrist John White writes in *Masks of Melancholy* (InterVarsity Press, 1982):

An . . . area where the pastoral counselor can offer help . . . is to teach and to encourage the sufferers in solid, inductive Bible study . . . Years ago, when I was seriously depressed, the thing that saved my own sanity was a dry-as-dust grappling with Hosea's prophecy. I spent weeks, morning by morning, making meticulous notes, checking historical allusions in the text. Slowly I began to sense the ground under my feet growing steadily firmer. I knew without any doubt that healing was constantly springing from my struggle to grasp the meaning of the prophecy.

There are several other approaches the Christian worker can employ to hasten the healing process. Scripture verses can be taped to noticeable places—the bathroom mirror, the refrigerator, the dashboard of the car. Pertinent sections of Scripture should be read over and over, even memorized, so that they become a part of the thought processes of the abuse victim. Here are some examples of relevant Scriptures:

1. To help with anxiety:
   Philippians 4:6
   Matthew 6:28-32
2. To help with guilt:
   I John 1:9, 10
   I John 2:1, 2
   Isaiah 43:25
3. To help experience God's love:
   Romans 5:4, 5
   I John
   John 15
4. To help gain assurance of salvation:
   Romans 10:9-11
   John 3:16
5. To help develop a sense of worth as a person:
   Psalm 139

I ask the counselee to write out these sections by hand and place them in obvious locations. The process of writing the words helps give a sense of ownership of the promises to the copyist.

Another Scriptural tool I find to be effective is an old study form called Christic meditation. This means that a person puts himself or herself into an incident from the Bible and imagines the circumstances as though he or she were actually present. Many women who have been abused have difficulty relating in a personal and intimate sense to God. The Gospel of Luke is particularly helpful because of the way it reveals Christ's relationship with women. For example, the abuse survivor may choose an incident like the one found in Luke 8:40-48 which deals with the woman suffering from a 12-year emission of blood. Then he or she should do the following exercises:

Describe the setting.

What kind of day is it?

What are the people wearing?

What is the weather like?
What does Jesus look like?
Who is accompanying Him?
What is wrong with you?
What do you need from Jesus?
What do you decide to do?
What fears do you have?
Why are you afraid?
How do you approach Him?
What happens?
What does He say to you?
What is the look in His eyes like?
How do you feel when you hear His voice?
What do His words mean to you?
What is happening to you?
What will you remember from this incident for the rest of your life?

This exercise personalizes Scripture and allows the Holy Spirit to make applications to the victim's spirit and mind which can be surprising in their immediacy and intimacy. When we work through one of these portions together, I ask that she go through the whole Book of Luke, placing herself in each event and allowing the Scriptural realities to become hers.

4. THE NEED TO WRITE

Another powerful tool I suggest is the process of writing. I ask those who come to me for help to begin to write down their thoughts. This can take the form of letters—letters to me, to the perpetrator of abuse, to husbands, to friends. These letters could be mailed, but they don't have to be. Or this writing can be in the form of poetry or a journal. The purpose is to regularly record thoughts that relate to past abuse and its present effect on the life of the survivor. I always promise to read anything that is sent to me.

There are several immediate benefits from this process. First of all, writing requires a discipline that speaking does not. The writer is forced to put thoughts on paper and mentally edit what is written. "Do I really mean that word?" " Is this really what happened?" "Have I expressed this as well as possible?" The writing process forces definition; the writer must define what he or she is thinking, feeling, and experiencing. Secondly, writing slows the process of living to such an extent that we must consider it, examine it, and be quiet to think. Finally, by writing these things, we are given a chronicle of our experiences. We begin to make connections and remember the events that would have passed from memory. The "why" questions of living begin to make some sense; we can begin to take responsibility for who we are.

I watched this process in the life of a woman who had been in therapy for several years. She seemed stuck, and I was about to recommend that she find another therapist. For some reason, she began to write letters to her therapist, and her therapy suddenly became directive, specific, and effective. She began to dream in ways that helped her realize what was buried in her subconscious. The letter writing not only helped her progress, but it helped her therapist better understand her psychological needs. He encouraged her to continue this discipline. She wrote the therapist several times each week. This enabled him to establish specific agendas for each session.

5. THE NEED TO LISTEN TO GOD

This same type of discipline can be used in prayer to the divine Counselor. I like to set aside a time of quiet, followed by asking the question "What do you have to say to me today, Lord?" In the beginning, two or three minutes of quiet may be all that is possible, but ten to fifteen minutes are ideal. One then listens with inner ears to whatever God brings to his or her consciousness. When the mind wanders, gently bring it back to attention. I write down the mundane thoughts that float to the surface during these quiet times. The columns of my prayer journal are crowded with "profound" messages such as "Take meat out of the freezer" or "Move the laundry." It helps me as I "listen" to focus on a symbol for God. Christ said that He was the Living Water so I might think of water flowing from a fountain—its refreshing qualities, the light sparkling on its surface, its coolness on the tongue. When my mind wanders, I bring it back to this symbol.

People ask me how I learned to recognize the inner voice of the Lord. My reply is that sometimes I don't. But most of the time it is like entering a crowded room, hearing someone laugh, and knowing that a well-loved friend is near because of the familiarity that has developed.

6. THE NEED FOR THE BODY OF CHRIST—THE CHURCH

There should be no place where healing occurs more thoroughly and acceptance felt more quickly than in the Church. The abused need to be embraced and nurtured by the body of Christ. The Church and God's people have much to offer those who have been so rudely mistreated.

Lay workers or vocational ministers must understand that everything they do can be a means of mediating the living Christ to a survivor suffering the effects of abuse. Touch, when it is holy, gentle, and unobtrusive, can be Christ's touch. Many abuse survivors are confused about touch. Some understand it only in a twisted sexual context. Some are afraid of human touch; it has only been abusive and brought pain. Some need desperately to be touched and held; they are starving for healthy human physical love. It is necessary to insert the caution again, that this special use of touch as means of mediating Christ must be done with great care when helping the opposite sex.

Often I find that as I work with the abused, their pain becomes my own in ways that can be deeply distressing. Because of this I, too, need to feel a healing touch of love given in the name of Christ. I am grateful that the church we attend includes "passing of the peace" each Sunday. We shake hands and embrace one another with pure hearts. Speaking God's peace to each other is another means by which the abused can experience God's holy love mediated through human acts.

The sacraments or ordinances of the Church have an ability, though often overlooked, to impart comfort to the participants. David Seamonds, a pastor and author of *Healing for Damaged Emotions* and *The Healing of Memories* (Victor Books, 1985) told in a lecture how he is more and more offering Communion privately to those with whom he counsels. Dr. Bill Wilson, formerly a professor of psychology at Duke University, explained to me the group therapy approach he uses with Christian homosexuals, many of whom began their gender confusion due to incestuous experiences. After several sessions, he always brings them to a place in which they participate in a Communion service which symbolizes partaking in the life of Christ.

People in distress should be taught to receive the bread and wine with expectation. The Holy Spirit will apply participation in the Lord's Supper in ways that touch the deepest needs. I regularly ask those people with whom I counsel, "How often are you taking Communion?'' I recommend that they participate as often as possible. This institution of the Christian Church was established as a memorial to Christ's death and resurrection, looking to the past and the future. But through the centuries it has also been a means of mediating holiness to countless seeking Christians. We need to reemphasize its healing potential to those in need.

The victim of abuse needs desperately to establish spiritual connections through the ministries of the Church, through acts of forgiveness, and other spiritual resources. These people need to cleanse their minds from the influences of the past by saturating them in Scripture; they need to experience the reality of the Word; they need to join the body of Christ through prayer, by sharing their burdens with others, and by knowing that friends love them enough not only to help but to hold them accountable. These are all viable tools which the nonprofessional counselor can offer. These are also tools that the Christian professional psychologist needs to integrate into therapy.

The people of God *can and must* help the victims of abuse toward wholeness.

Chapter 5

The Need for Awareness

According to current statistics, it is possible that as many as one fourth of the women sitting in church on any Sunday morning have been abused in some way. Countless women and children never know what will happen to them once the batterer—the husband or father—comes home and the doors are closed. This tragedy demands our attention.

In this increasingly violent culture, the Christian Church must formulate loving policies of intervention and advocacy in order to bring healing, redemption, and hope to situations of family pain. Christians first must be informed and then activated to bring a halt to abusive cycles that permeate our society.

How does the local church go about informing its membership of the need for involvement? How can policies be established? Where do we begin? The purpose of this chapter is to answer these questions.

A good place to begin informing a church is to plan an awareness meeting. Here are the kinds of things this meeting should include:

What We Must Know

Christians must understand that the effects of abuse are not limited to the duration of the abuse, but manifest themselves well into adult life. This means that it is not enough just to stop injustices that go on within a family; but love, support, and spiritual guidance must be shown to a person who has been abused as he or she works toward emotional and psychological wholeness.

This was demonstrated by a letter I received from a man in his seventies who wrote that he had finally been able to forgive his father who, when he was a child, had forced him into homosexual acts. He wrote, ''I cannot tell you what it was like. For the first time in my life I was able to actually *feel* God's love! It flowed through me and overflowed me. It was like I was sitting

71

in a pool of light.'' Abuse that had occurred decades earlier had hindered this man from experiencing God's love most of his life.

An example of members of a Christian community helping to stop abuse is found in Kathy Miller's book *Out of Control: A Christian Parent's Victorious Struggle over Child Abuse* (Word Books). In it she writes how she struggled to overcome abusive behavior toward her own child. She tells how she came to terms with her anger through the prayers of a group of women, their parenting advice, and an older Christian woman who made herself available when Kathy's home situation got rough. The actions she used to modify her angry, abusive behavior came from Christian books and from parenting advice she had been given. But the courage to make the necessary changes came because of the love and support of godly women.

The Facets of Abuse

A good place for the education of the Church to begin is to learn to recognize the forms abuse can take. Six types of abusive behavior have been outlined by Parents Anonymous, a crisis intervention program designed to help parents control abusive behavior. They are as follows:

1. *Physical abuse*. Inflicting or causing injury to a person, other than accidentally.

2. *Physical neglect*. Failing to provide proper food, clothing, medical care, parental guidance or supervision.

3. *Sexual abuse*. Committing any type of sexual act with a child or failure to stop such action from occurring.

4. *Verbal abuse*. Using insulting, crude, or foul language toward a person; a continued habit of harsh scolding.

5. *Emotional abuse*. Maintaining a negative atmosphere that causes a child to feel inadequate, inferior, or unimportant.

6. *Emotional neglect*. Failing to provide a nurturing emotional atmosphere for a child; showing no feeling for a child.

This description of abuses provides a foundation from which to educate the supportive community of the Church. Christian education needs to be expanded to equip the Christian home with the ability to counter domestic injustice. The Church must be equipped to undertake parental and marital training.

When dealing with the abused, concern for the victim must be kept in tension with concern for the victimizer. The battered person needs loving intervention; but the parent or spouse who loses control of his or her behavior also needs help in order to stop destructive habits and replace them with positive behavior.

Consider this situation of wife battering. A woman was giving a birthday party for her child which included neighborhood children and their mothers. Her husband returned home from work, took her into the bedroom, slapped her, ripped her clothes, threw her to the floor, and tried to force her into bed to have sex with him. Weeping, she pleaded with him to stop because of the party going on in the basement. He responded by telling everyone to go home. Then he got a knife from the kitchen, forced her to bed, and had intercourse with her. "My nose was still bleeding," she said.

What could have been done in this situation? If you had been one of the mothers attending the party, would you have been prepared to intervene? Would you have been able to refer this couple to an area crisis center? There are now over 800 shelters in the United States to protect battered wives who are like prisoners in their own homes. The first such shelter opened more than 20 years ago in a private home in Pasadena, California. There are also about 50 programs for the abusive male, the first having been established in Boston in 1977. Do you know how to contact the centers in your area?

In the case study of Timothy Martin (see Chapter 3), Pat Meyer's prayerful intervention demonstrated a concern for his entire family. She was not simply angry about Timothy's neglect, she was able to identify with the needs of each member of the family. She had compassion for his older sister because Pat could remember herself in that same position. She sensitively related to Timothy's father, understanding that, though he felt his family life was failing, his ego didn't need additional blows from outsiders. Pat organized a committee of caring people in such a way that the Martin family never felt like they had become a "project."

In this situation, indirect pressure was put on the abuser—the mother—to help her see her problem. Direct intervention, such as legally removing the abuser from the home, is often needed when violence or incest occurs.

Alcohol and Abuse

As has been seen in the case study of Timothy Martin, excessive consumption of alcohol can contribute to abuse in the home. Abuse and alcohol frequently are companion problems. It is important for the Church to be aware of this and the effect alcoholism can have on the dynamics of a family.

Children of the alcoholic are prime candidates for abuse and neglect. Early in life, these children develop coping strategies (as do all who suffer from abuse). They may learn to get attention by misbehaving because negative attention seems better to them than no attention. Or they may assume adultlike attitudes, emotions, and responsibilities, forfeiting their own childhood.

Coming from every socioeconomic level, ethnic and religious group, children of alcoholics have had unusual demands placed on their lives. Avis Brenner of Boston's Lesley College, founder of the Child and Community Program which works with children under stress, has described these unreasonable demands in her book *Helping Children Cope with Stress* (Lexington Books, 1984). The communication in an alcoholic home is full of confusing messages. Here is a summary of these kinds of messages:

These children hear: *Don't tell!* This may be accompanied by a variety of rationalizations such as "Your dad has been working hard lately" or "Your mother is upset because of Grandma." This deliberate habit of lying poses a constant struggle with reality for the child who wants to love his parents but must cope with the glaring hypocrisy of their lives.

These children hear: *Take care of me!* Most often the adult, unable to take responsibility for his or her own life, imposes upon the child responsibilities they have shunned—from caring for siblings to lying to the boss about work absences.

These children hear: *It's your fault! Cope! Just cope!* Soon these children assume the blame of their parents' guilt. They learn to cope in different ways. One child may try to be *superkid*, a perfect, flawless child or adolescent; another may be *placater*, the arbitrator between Mom and Dad, Mom and the world, or Dad and the family; another may be *adjuster*, a child who goes with the flow but never learns to confront his or her own feelings as the parents' demands are met; yet another may be an *alley kid*, the potential delinquent who tries to take on other kids, school authorities, and the whole world.

These children hear: *Don't feel!* And they learn not to feel as they go through life. They have learned that to feel is to hurt—to know the pain of rejection.

If there were ever an opportunity to exemplify Christlike love, it is to children who are being abused at the hand of people who should be protecting, sheltering, and nurturing them—their parents. And it is often through giving love to these children that the parents are also reached with the message of Christ's love.

How great is the effect of alcohol on the family, and does the problem filter into the Church? The problem is great, and, yes, the Church is affected. One fourth of a sample population surveyed in a 1978 Gallop Poll admitted that use of alcohol had negatively affected their family life. But only eight percent of all surveyed said they would turn for help to the Church or its personnel.

Jeffrey VanVonderen, in *Good News for the Chemically Dependent* (Thomas Nelson Publishers, 1985), described the presence of drinking problems in churches in the United States:

> In churches where drinking is approached very conservatively (as a sin), half as many people drink as in those that hold a more liberal view (a matter of personal choice). Yet, in the conservative churches, of those who choose to drink anyway, twice as many develop alcohol-related problems. That means that the number of problem drinkers is the same in both kinds of churches.
>
> Chemical dependency is a problem that has reached epidemic proportions in our society. . . . Holding a religious view that prohibits alcohol use proves no more effective in the area of preventing chemical-related problems than holding a liberal view.

The church has a responsibility to reach into society and help those who are substance dependent. It also has a responsibility to educate itself and its members on the far-reaching ramifications of this problem and to begin working with those suffering from the effects of chemical addiction. Only three percent of all alcoholics are in skid row settings; 97 percent are moms and dads, teachers, lawyers, doctors, pastors, cheerleaders, and Sunday school superintendents—family type people holding down jobs. Family relationships have a tendency to disintegrate sooner than professional relationships because the alcoholic tends to hide his or her addiction and to find affirmation there.

Awareness and Intervention

Many people find the thought of trying to help a battering situation to be uncomfortable, much less a case of incest. The taboo nature of these acts lends a repugnance to the situations so that many Christians would rather deny existence of these problems than become involved with them. The Church needs to educate compassionate people to the steps that must be taken to help victims of these injustices so that God's people can reach out with confidence and knowledge.

Because people involved in other people's lives (like youth workers, Sunday School teachers, small group leaders, etc.) often are first to become aware of abuse situations, church workers need to know procedures to follow when intervention is needed. Help in establishing these guidelines may be obtained by consulting models used by local public schools. This information then can be adapted to the needs of the local church.

Once a procedure for intervention is established, the congregation needs to be made aware of symptoms or signs that abuse may be occurring. *Youthworker* (Winter, 1985) magazine gives a list of warning signs that may indicate a sexually abusive environment. This comprehensive guideline is helpful for Christian workers who are responsible for ministering to youth. It also has implications for family and children's ministries.

Family characteristics:
- poor parental models
- isolated family with shallow interpersonal relationships
- unrealistic expectations for the children
- absence of one parent due to divorce or illness
- alcoholism or substance abuse
- silence on or conflicting views about sex
- father ruling household by fear and friction
- child assuming adult responsibility in home
- intense family conflict
- secretiveness among family members

Victims' social behavior:
- states or implies sexual activity
- sexual knowledge or activity inappropriate to the age (excessive masturbation, promiscuity, seductive activity)
- fear of specific persons or situations or being alone
- refraining from physical activities
- hides, runs away, truancy
- no close friends
- constant private companionship with a specific older person

Victims emotional responses:
- fear and mistrust of others
- extreme secrecy about menstrual cycle and sexual issues

- daydreaming or fantasizing
- aloofness or withdrawal
- severe change in grades
- excessive expression of guilt and perfectionism
- depression
- fear of medical examinations or physical exposure
- expressions of perceived uncleanliness, such as excessive bathing

Physical signs of abuse:
- frequent headaches, stomachaches, vomiting
- unwanted pregnancy without revealing the identity of the father
- venereal disease
- constant infections, bruises, bleeding
- self-destructive behavior (attempted suicide, frequent accidents, drug or alcohol abuse)
- excessive weight change

Spiritual indications of abuse:
- difficulty trusting God the Father
- difficulty understanding and accepting forgiveness, expressed as constant guilt
- judgmental attitude toward self and others
- always trying to please God and spiritual leaders
- difficulty with obedience to parents
- struggle with discipline

Used by permission. © 1985, Alice Huskey

Becoming aware of the extent of sexual abuse can be overwhelming. Imagine the dilemma of the public schoolteacher who attended my workshop on abuse. She related to me that, as required, she had taken her early grade school class through a curriculum entitled *Good Touch: Bad Touch*. She discovered that 14 students in her class of 32 indicated sexual abuse happening within their homes. After interviewing each child privately, according to an established procedure, she was convinced each child was describing actual occurrences. It is not likely that many Sunday School classes would show comparable results, but it does indicate that abuse can occur more frequently than most of us would expect.

Each of those children in that classroom needed to be believed by the teacher—believed that what he or she said had happened was true. Teachers in private and public schools are legally mandated to report cases of suspected child abuse. All 50 states have statutes requiring certain professionals to report suspected incidents of physical and sexual abuse as well as physical and emotional neglect. Some states, such as New York, require that public schools teach students in kindergarten through sixth grade about sexual abuse.

To say "I believe you" in these cases in the public schools means that there must be:

1. Mechanisms through which the school cooperates with local child protections agencies.
2. A workable reporting procedure that protects the rights and responsibilities of staff members.
3. Staff to provide administrative support for policy mandates.
4. Documentation strategies.
5. A sense of responsibility of school personnel after reporting cases of maltreatment.

Public education is becoming involved in abuse. What about the Church?

We Christian leaders need to hear our children, teens, spouses, and friends with believing ears. The ministering person must work through his or her own attitudes of denial, horror, and sexuality. Many female victims will not go to their pastors for help with sexual abuse because they fear disbelief, lack of understanding, insensitivity, etc. A woman often provides more sympathy. But, unfortunately, few local churches provide competent women counselors.

Marie Marshall Fortune in *Sexual Violence: The Unmentionable Sin* (Pilgrim Press, 1983) recommends that a minister should be aware of his own feelings regarding sexual violence. He must look for hidden stereotypes he might have (such as one that suggests an adolescent girl probably enticed her father into incest). He also must be in touch with his own reactions to sexual violence. Were there similar experiences in his own background that make the victim's story more repugnant to him?

To say "I believe you" can be much more complicated than just speaking the words because unbelieving actions can negate any positive effect of what has been spoken. To work with victims of incest means that one must be prepared to hear stories that seem unbelievable. It was difficult for one pastor I know to be told by a teenaged runaway that she had left home because her father, the Sunday School superintendent (or the head of the seminary Bible department, or whoever), was sexually abusing her.

The Church must realize how difficult the life journey is for the victims of incest. Everything in their world has been disordered. They may be unable to relate to father as father, or brother as brother because father may have become lover or brother become boyfriend. These children have been violated in every way. Their bodies have been used, their minds wrenched, and their emotions suppressed. Each of them has been robbed of a sense of self, a sense of family, a sense of proper sex roles, a sense of security and trust. One woman with a history of long-term incest said she felt like she wore a sign around her neck which declared "Used. Abused. Misuse me, please." Her present relationships replicated the unhealthy relationships of the past.

Should a child be enticed into sex play by an older stepbrother, a scenario may go like this. The boy spends lots of private time with the child. This soon leads to caressing and fondling. Sessions of foreplay follow, genital exploration, and finally intercourse. All the while, the child is in emotional bondage to the older boy; she is under the power of another who has ruthlessly used her for his own purpose. "You started it," he whispers. "You want me to do this to you." She is entrapped and begins to believe his words.

Most incest victims need professional help because of the ways in which incestuous acts disorder the survivor's context of reality. Sexual abuse can badly distort an individual's concept of himself or herself. Mistrust, anger, guilt, fear, depression, feeling unclean and used, lack of self-control, low self-esteem, poor social skills, sexual role confusion, sexual dysfunction are only a few of the problems with which a victim must contend.

Psychologist David Elkind, who wrote *All Grown Up and No Place to Go* (Addison-Wesley Publishing, 1984), describes the effect of incest in this way:

Incest is a barrier to discovering the self, for it embeds in the person a sense of being vulnerable, of not really being in charge of the only thing we really have charge of, namely, our bodies. Once we understand the pain of incest, we can understand also why some young people want to adopt a ready-made substitute identity, such as those provided by cults.

Incest can badly distort a person's concept of God. When a father or a trusted male figure has abused a child, the victim develops fear and anxiety toward men. This is transferred, often unknowingly, to the divine patriarchal figure, God, our Heavenly Father. An incest survivor expresses this feeling well in a poem entitled "God" from the book *Silent Scream* by Martha Janssen (Fortress Press, 1983).

GOD
I've been glad for God the Spirit,
and for God the Son
because I don't believe
my heart can ever understand
that God
is like a father.

Because of the nature of problems that result from prolonged incest, the person who first learns of the situation is often called upon to refer the victim to people trained in psychological intervention. Professionals maintain that the most important measurement by which to judge the skills of a therapist is not whether or not he or she is a Christian, but if the therapist is an expert. The ideal, of course, is a Christian counselor who specializes in helping the abused and who integrates spiritual truth with psychological understanding. But, as in many professions, some non-Christian therapists are more proficient than Christians.

It must be pointed out that some practitioners in mental health fields are hostile to the Christian faith. I tell those seeking professional help to be open with a prospective counselor about their beliefs—the centrality of Christ in their lives. They should simply ask the therapist if he or she will be amenable to working within the framework of those beliefs. Not only does the professional interview the client by taking a case history, but the abuse victim should interview the professional to be sure they can work well together.

Preventative Awareness

Prevention strategies are perhaps the most effective area in which the lay worker can be involved. One important deterrent to sexual abuse is educating the child. Tragically, most parents talk to their children about sexual assault after it has happened.

In this day, sex education means that a parent must become explicit, giving proper names to all parts of the body. It is important to inform the child that not everyone will want to do what is best for him or her. A parent must learn to say: "Some people want to touch children in ways that they shouldn't." "Sometime someone may want to touch your vagina (or penis), and you don't want them to. Tell him to stop it!" "Sometime someone might try to make you touch his penis, and you don't want to. Remember, say 'No! Don't do that to me!' " A parent should add, "If this ever happens to you, tell me about it right away."

Experts point out that a man who makes advances to a small child may actually be aroused by his victim's fearful compliance; but he may be effectively put off by a child who is able to say boldly, "Don't do that! I don't like that!" Simple verbal defenses can be a significant defense against attempted assault. It is important to underline the fact that the "someone" who might want the child to do such things might be a friend, a neighbor, a family member, or a familiar authority. This kind of education requires sensitivity and care so that an unhealthy fear of people is not instilled in young children.

Excellent educational tools are available for teaching children about abuse in positive ways. Lists of these resources should be made and distributed at awareness meetings. Here are some examples (see Bibliography for a more complete listing):

Little Ones Teaching Kit by Lynn Heitritter does an excellent job providing the information children need on sexual abuse. The activity workbook provides pages to color, definitions, and Scripture verses. It also includes instructions to train the child about "good touches," "bad touches," and how to use God's gift of the mind—"the thinker." It is accompanied by a parent's teaching guide by William Katz entitled *Protecting Your Children from Sexual Assault*. These can be ordered from:

Christian Society for Prevention of Cruelty to Children
8200 Grand Avenue South
Bloomington, Minnesota 55420

Another good resource is *Scared, but Not Too Scared* by Dave Jackson (David C. Cook Publishing, 1985). This book teaches children ways of coping with a variety of frightening situations.

Many "touch" curricula are being developed for school programs. One of the best known is sponsored by Illusion Theater based in Minneapolis. Its play *Touch* has been seen by more than

450,000 students in 35 states. Concerned people in local churches may want to review some of these curricula to decide if any would be appropriate for church education sessions.

Another educational aid is "Caring for the Victims" by George H. Perry. This includes "Speak Up! Say No!" a cartoon filmstrip for preschoolers and kindergartners, "Child Molestation: When to Say No" for elementary school children, "Shatter the Silence," a film for adolescents, and "Child Sexual Abuse: The Untold Secret" a videocassette presentation for junior and senior high school students.

Ways to Inform

Here are some goals you might want to accomplish in an awareness meeting. These are ways the local church can become a healing advocate for abuse victims.

FORM A TASK FORCE ON ABUSE

Work that is done by people who feel strongly about their task will be accomplished effectively. A handful of concerned lay people can educate themselves regarding the dynamics of abuse in our culture so that they, in turn, can educate a local congregation. Perhaps there are some who have survived a background of abuse who will want to bring their experiential sensitivity to this task. Once education has been accomplished, a church then can begin to formulate policies.

Commission lay people to:
• Determine what helping agencies exist in your local community and which services are lacking.
• List hot line abuse numbers for victims to call.
• List shelters (with addresses) for battered wives and sexual assault counseling centers.
• Identify which local counselors and therapists are experienced in abuse cases. Discover counselors who work with the abusive male.
• Research preventative measures to teach children and families how to protect themselves from abuse. Adapt appropriate material for church seminars.
• Discover teaching materials which could be used in the home.
• Make the bibliography from this book available for further research on this topic.

Commission this task force to present information from this

book to guide the church staff and lay workers in formulating sensitive, compassionate policies for helping intrafamily abuse situations. Invite this commission to make a formal educational report to the staff and lay governing body along with recommendations of ministries for the abused.

ENCOURAGE WOMEN TO REDESIGN MINISTRIES FOR WOMEN

Centuries ago, Euripides said that women are a woman's greatest ally. Since 1970, it has been women who have sponsored public forums on topics relating to domestic violence and sexual abuse. The Child Protection Lobby has created a professional and moral legitimacy for open discussion of sexuality. This coalition is concerned with sexual dysfunction and the incidence and effect of violence to women and children. The power of the Child Protection Lobby has increased in recent years because physicians have joined the ranks of a group that once was a group largely composed of social workers.

Actions of secular groups have brought the injustices of private abuse to national consciousness. Discussions of approaches to bring about healing are taking place in the United States, but often these groups tend toward a humanistic orientation. Christian input is desperately needed at all levels of intervention for the effects of intrafamily abuse. If that is not forthcoming, a vacuum will be created into which others will step; in fact, a vacuum exists now because of our reluctance to become interested in this problem.

It is especially important for women to be involved in policy making and establishment of programs that minister to women. Few male-dominated church executive boards appear to be able to do for women what needs to be done. Therefore, invite gifted women to compassionately and pragmatically redesign the church's outreach to women. Ask them to carefully investigate the needs of women within the geographic area of the church. Then evaluate existing programs to determine if current needs are being met or if new ministries should be established.
Is there a need for:
• A divorce recovery group?
• A preventative maintenance program for married couples?
• More emphasis on the Christian philosophy of individual self-esteem and family well-being?
• A nurturing group for young parents?

- Elective parenting classes—mornings for women at home, evenings for working women?
- Mentoring by older women who could become surrogate extended family members?

Each of these suggestions could become means for breaking existing abusive cycles or sources for education that could prevent abuse from starting. Key aspects to these programs would be unconditional acceptance and support for each participant, affirmation of the value of each individual, provision of Christ-centered instruction on relationships within the family, and help to be able to forgive self and others. Programs of these types can become instruments in the ministry of reconciliation—reconciliation to God, to family members, and to self.

CONDUCT A SELF-EXAMINATION

Abuse is self-perpetuating. Ignorance about the subtle forms of abuse may be harmful because it can allow abuse to infiltrate relationships unchecked—just because it doesn't seem blatant or physically harmful. Consider distributing this list of questions during the awareness meeting because every Christian worker or minister needs to examine himself or herself in the light of these discussions on abuse.

- Do I devalue my spouse verbally—using humiliating put-downs, subtle, ego-deflating name-calling, humorous one-liners that focus on stupidity or ineptitude?
- Have I ever struck my spouse, pushed, or intimidated him or her? Have I ever thrown things or pushed furniture?
- Do I "whip" my wife with the doctrine of submission?
- Do I "hit" my husband at his points of weakness?
- Do I "pound" my children with the concept of parental authority?
- Do I ever scream and shout, rage and fume?
- Do I, maybe subconsciously, think women are inferior?
- What is my attitude toward my home and the people living in it?
- Is my attitude toward both sexes formed by my parents' marriage which may have been unhealthy?
- Could my children someday say, "I never really felt Dad's (or Mom's) love"?

Sometimes fleeting glimpses of our own human nature remind us that all of us need God's continuing work of redemption.

ADDRESS THE ISSUE OF ABUSE FROM THE PULPIT

The problem of abuse is so widespread in the United States that it has become a major social issue. The pulpit, which has always been the ethical and moral voice of our nation, must begin to address the issues of abuse—the maltreatment of women and children. Paul Simmons, the pastor in the fictionalized case study of wife battering, found this emphasis necessary and helpful in his ministry. A practical theological perspective needs to be developed to help lay people realize the effects of abuse in their own lives and help them combat it in society from a Christian perspective.

Several things might be helpful for the average congregation:

- A series of sermons on a Christian perspective toward abuse—including respect for and the value of the individual.
- A report to the congregation on the findings of the lay task force on abuse.
- Testimonies from those from a background of abuse who are healed enough to teach and help others based on their own experience.
- A panel of professionals who work with the abused to give insight into conditions and prevalence of intrafamily abuse and the help that is available for abuse survivors.
- Support groups for abuse survivors and their families or friends.

BEGIN FAITHFUL PRAYER INTERCESSION FOR THE ABUSED

Abuse is a work of the enemy and will require faithful, consistent intercessory prayer. I John 3:8 (RSV) says: "The reason the Son of God appeared was to destroy the works of the devil." There are many reasons for the Incarnation of Christ. One of them is destruction of the work of the enemy of our souls.

This also is work of the Church. Nothing destroys the exquisite beauty of God's image within humanity more than abuse. We must never forget this is a spiritual work. We can organize, educate, and become involved; but unless we pray, the enemy will hold tightly and be reluctant to release its victims.

Once a week, I find a personal sanctuary where I can spend time to pray without interruption. For those moments I give myself to be an intercessor for those who, in the words of an old prayer, are "held in bitter thralldoms." Though I am by myself, I often sense that I am not alone spiritually. Hundreds of other intercessors, unseen and unknown by me, are making themselves available to Christ as He destroys the works of the Devil. But if these supernatural wars are to be waged successfully, we must be joined by thousands more.

Over and over I pray this prayer for each abuse victim who finds her way to my door, to our ministry, or to my phone:

My Lord Jesus,
You were wounded for each one of us.
May the blood from Your wounds be poured like a healing ointment into the wounds of this one I love.
May this one experience cleansing, release, freedom from bondage, a great new life—and finally joy!
I have faith that You will answer this prayer because I know it is Your desire, as it is mine.
I love You, wounded Healer.
Be health now for my friend.
In Christ's name. Amen.

In addition to praying that personal prayer, I sent the following prayer to hundreds of people across the United States who wrote to our broadcast regarding their own experiences with abuse. I invited these people to join me as intercessors in an ongoing vigil. This prayer may be reproduced so it can be available to anyone who wishes to intercede on behalf of the abused.

In the name of Jesus Christ and through His act of love at Calvary, I refuse the power of the enemy who seeks to destroy life. I speak life in the very name of Christ who is the One who is the way, the truth, and the life.

Together, with my brothers and sisters, in spiritual union, I bind the powers of darkness and pray that the light of Heaven will shine in this terrible gloom. Beneath the shadow of Christ's cross and through the power of the Holy Spirit, we request that abusers, even now, will be prevented in their acts and that victims will be protected.

We commit ourselves as intercessors for our sorry nation and give ourselves to this prayer vigil each time we hear of abuse or remember our own pain or the pain of one we love. Help us thereby to use the very act of the enemy against us as an act of redemption in the life of another. Heal us, O God, with Your powerful works of love.

In Christ's name. Amen.

CHAPTER 6

THEORY AND THEOLOGY
OF ABUSE

ONE DAY, WHEN MY HUSBAND WAS A YOUNG MINISTER serving in the heart of Chicago, we were walking with friends in a neighborhood near our home. One friend suddenly said, "Hey! Hugh Hefner's mansion is somewhere around here." Interested in catching a glimpse of the home of the *Playboy* empire's founder, my husband stopped a passing stranger. "Do you know where the Hefner mansion is?" David asked.

The young man gave us directions and said, "Yes, that's where 'god' lives."

Climate for Abuse

Hugh Hefner, and many like him, are demigods of the sexual revolution who defy the Christian ethics of monogamy, fidelity, and sexual purity. They have laid a foundation of permissiveness upon which much of the sexual violence that exists in our culture and in our private lives has been constructed. When I think about these people, I think of the prophet Isaiah warning, "Woe to those who call evil good and good evil, who put darkness for light and light for darkness, who put bitter for sweet and sweet for bitter!" (Isa. 5:20, RSV).

Despite propaganda for personal sexual freedom ("Do what feels good to you!"), narcissism, and promises of exciting, illicit activities, promoters of hedonism have created a climate for abuse which has caused untold suffering. No discussion of the causes of abuse could be complete without placing domestic violence in its proper context—a sexually permissive society. We cannot measure the cost of emotional and psychological suffering which has accompanied the contemporary sexual revolution.

The prophet Isaiah wrote, "For wickedness burns like a fire, it consumes briers and thorns; it kindles the thickets of the forest, and they roll upward in a column of smoke . . . the land is burned, and the people are like fuel for the fire'' (Isa. 9:18, 19, RSV).

Pornography is a prime contributor to the climate of abuse. The estimated six-billion-dollar sex industry has been slickly packaged, but its effect in terms of suffering of the innocent cannot be glossed over. Contrary to past legal decisions regarding pornography, some experts in the social sciences are showing pornography to be a major influence on abuse in the United States.

Shirley O'Brien, Human Development Specialist at the University of Arizona, wrote that when most child molesters are arrested, child pornography is also confiscated. Police vice squads report that 77 percent of molesters of boys and 87 percent of molesters of girls admit imitating sexual behavior they have seen modeled in pornography. In one group of rapists questioned, 57 percent indicated they had tried sexual activity they had seen depicted by pornography.

What are the porno industry's plans for the future? There is nothing secret or hidden about its intentions. We can expect more of what we already have available in our communities, including homosexual and deviant pornography. In the future, however, technology will make obscene material more accessible through the home video cassette recorders and cable television markets.

How has the pornography industry grown to such proportions? How has domestic violence become so widespread? The answer to both questions is that *we have become morally desensitized.* The issues that once outraged us outrage us no more.

The most influential and effective demoralizer, is found in most of our homes—the great ''god'' television. This ''shrine'' sits in 99 percent of American homes and is ''worshiped'' by an adoring public on the average of 44 hours per week.

What is the relationship of viewing television to violence and to abuse?

How does moral desensitization work? Researchers are finding that television is the perfect tool. Behavior-modification therapists use desensitization techniques to adjust unacceptable behavior in patients. In an unpublished master's level research paper, Richard L. Fredericks describes the desensitization process. He refers to the work of Dr. Joseph Wolpe, and expert in behavior modification. Wolpe wrote, ''Systematic desensitization is most effective when done with images . . . in a nonthreatening environment.''

The process used by behavior-modification therapists to assist patients in altering negative behavior patterns uses six steps. The application to television viewing is obvious:

1. The person views familiar images in a comfortable, nonthreatening situation. He is completely relaxed. No emotional arousal is noted.

2. Certain images or scenes known to arouse emotional reactions are introduced. The patient's relaxation ceases.

3. The scene shifts or viewing is interrupted. The viewer's emotion's are not given time to react.

4. The viewer is given a respite period of approximately one minute during which he resumes a relaxed mental and physical state. This is facilitated by eating or drinking.

5. As the viewer's emotions subside, the viewing of nonthreatening images resumes. The subject is completely relaxed. No strong feelings are noted by the therapist.

6. The cycle is repeated. Therapists who use systematic desensitization claim that it usually only requires only 20 to 30 exposure sessions to alter a person's feelings from acceptance to rejection—more importantly for the purposes of our discussion, from rejection to acceptance.

Since the 1950's television has enjoyed a luxury no behavior-modification therapist ever dreamed of having. It has been allowed to work its demoralizing effects in its subject's most relaxed, natural, and nonthreatening environment—his or her own home. But most of all, television has been allowed to rehearse its basic collection of themes over and over for each viewer—not 30 times but thousands of times, not in weekly therapy sessions but every day.

Drs. Linda and Robert Lichter of George Washington University conducted a study of crimes depicted on television. The study found that there are 1.7 crimes per show, more than two per hour. Murder was by far the most common crime on TV. Television crime is 100 times more likely to involve murder than real-life crime. While violent crime is only ten percent of real-life crime, it is 88 percent of TV crime.

The effect of this was summarized by comedian Red Skelton: "They sell violence. Now, they say this doesn't affect your mind in any way whatsoever; but if you can subliminally sell a product in 30 seconds, what does one hour of filth or violence do to your brain?''

Moreover, if negative behavior of a patient can be modified in 20 to 30 desensitization exposures, what can we conclude about moral desensitization of a person who spent his or her formative years viewing scenes of violence and degraded sexuality? Is it any wonder that people in the United States are exhibiting increased sexually aggressive behavior, especially toward women and young girls?

Since 1933, rape in the United States has increased more than 700 percent. This means that the chances of a woman being sexually assaulted are seven times greater than they were 50 years ago.

Alarming reports are being published regarding the content of television programming. Donald Wildmon of the National Federation for Decency stated that by the time a youngster graduates from high school, he or she will have watched an estimated 18,000 TV murders. According to the National Coalition of Television Violence, more than 2,000 studies confirm a relationship between viewing violence on a TV screen and instigating real violence.

Such is the climate in which we find ourselves, a climate which all too often encourages family abuse. What can God do in such a climate? What does He want us to do?

Need for Moral Sensitivity

It is high time that Christians began to be responsible. We must begin to develop the discipline to turn off our television sets, the prime source for the moral desensitization of our children and ourselves.

Our family has been without a television set since 1972. Considering current research, I am glad we made this drastic decision when we did. Our grown children now comment, ''I'm glad we didn't have a television while we were growing up.''

Controlling television viewing does not necessarily require getting rid of this technological phenomenon; it does mean developing stringent viewing habits and regularly reviewing what is watched. If you are unable to control the television in your home, perhaps you should get rid of it.

Sin has become a familiar companion. Alexander Pope once wrote in his *Essays on Man*:

Vice is a monster of so frightful mien;
As to be hated needs but to be seen;
Yet seen too oft, familiar with her face,
We first endure, then pity, then embrace.

We no longer view crime with a tender conscience. We no longer recoil with horror at violence. Too many of us have become hardened and greedy, with a clandestine interest in lewdness.

The Book of Judges tells us about the decline of morality in Israel.

And the people of Israel did what was evil in the sight of the Lord and served the Baals; and they forsook the Lord, the God of their fathers, who had brought them out of the land of Egypt; they went after other gods, from among the gods of the peoples who were round about them, and bowed down to them (Judges 2:11, 12, RSV).

How can the Church raise its voice and cry about the societal causes of abuse when there is an electronic shrine to the Baal of violence and sexual perversion in the home of most of its members? Let us hew down the family "altars" of television. If we do nothing, can *we* expect to escape the fierce anger of the Lord? It is only after we place private abuse in its public context that we can begin to develop a theological perspective on the topic.

The Work of God

Christ's declaration at the start of His ministry is like a proclamation of liberty and healing for the abused:

"The Spirit of the Lord is upon me, because he has anointed me to preach good news to the poor. He has sent me to proclaim release to the captives and recovering of sight to the blind, to set at liberty those who are oppressed, to proclaim the acceptable year of the Lord" (Luke 4:18, 19, RSV).

"He was despised and rejected by men, a man of sorrows and acquainted with grief . . . Surely he has born our griefs and carried our sorrows." This prophecy about the Messiah (Isaiah 53:3, 4, RSV) reminds us that Christ in His redemptive mission has taken all the sins of mankind upon Himself in order that we might be free from them. Knowing that, we can endure the waves of revulsion that overcome us as we hear stories of abuse.

91

When the reality of man's inhumanity to man, or man's inhumanity to woman, or woman's inhumanity to man comes crushing against us, we can look to Christ, to His cross, to His pierced hands and feet, and know that He has taken these agonies upon Himself. His blood was poured out for the remission of these inhuman blasphemies.

He has borne the griefs from the sins of incest, child abuse, other forms of family violence, and emotional and physical neglect. What a God is this—a Man of sorrows and acquainted with grief. This God understands and loves the abused and the abuser, even while He hates the abuse.

Those who have been abused or who deal with victims and perpetrators of abuse must understand that a theology of abuse begins at Christ's cross.

The Words of Christ

Christ's attitude toward women and children is a valuable model for us today. Much of the correction needed for domestic abuse within households of the Church might begin if we understood His approach and determined to be like Him as we relate to one another. We must teach His approach from our pulpits, from the lecterns of our classrooms, and in Bible study groups.

We need to remember that children are fragile and depend on adult protection. This canopy of security which we must provide for them is God-ordained. Most of us are woefully untrained for the responsibility of being a parent; our incomplete maturation complicates the task.

When I look through the lens of abuse at Christ's words regarding children and remember the precious fragility of a child's health and faith, I am amazed at the appropriateness of His words for our violent culture. ". . . whoever causes one of these little ones who believe in me to sin, it would be better for him to have a great millstone fastened round his neck and to be drowned in the depth of the sea" (Mt. 18:6, RSV).

Christ's warning is consistent with the Old Testament prohibitions regarding incest. Leviticus 18:6 reads: "None of you shall approach any one near of kin to him to uncover nakedness. I am the Lord." A comprehensive list follows which details those who are considered blood relatives. Leviticus 20:12 declares that death is the penalty for incest; Deuteronomy 27:22 pronounces a curse on the perpetrator.

Christ's teaching about children indicates that He considers them precious. As He addressed His disciples, He called a child to Himself and said:

"Truly, I say to you, unless you turn and become like children, you will never enter the kingdom of heaven. Whoever humbles himself like this child, he is the greatest in the kingdom of heaven.
Whoever receives one such child in my name receives me. See that you do not despise one of these little ones; for I tell you that in heaven their angels always behold the face of my Father who is in heaven. So it is not the will of my Father who is in heaven that one of these little ones should perish" (Mt. 18:3-5, 10, 14, RSV).

In the same way, Christ's attitude toward women should become the foundation for our understanding of male-female relationships.

When working with abuse victims, I attempt as soon as possible to introduce them to the male Christ, to help them experience this One who will never abuse them, force them, or twist their wills to devious purposes. This Man can spiritually fill the role of husband, friend, brother, father. His masculine qualities are perfectly balanced with feminine nurturing attributes. He can be strong and gentle; He can nurture tenderly, embrace without sexuality. He is perfectly trustworthy.

Jesus Christ is an advocate for women. Though many women have a difficult time learning that they can safely commit themselves to a relationship with the living Christ, once they begin to comprehend His beauty and purity, inner healing is hastened and spiritual health begins to flourish.

We must experience the reality of this Christ in such a way that He is able to transform our whole approach to male-female relationships. In your mind's eye, look at Him in the Scriptures:
—See His behavior toward women. He is tenderhearted toward the widow who lost a son. She is alone, with no visible means of support; even her husband's family name is dead. Jesus touches the bier and the son comes back to life.
—See a town whore embrace His feet before a room full of self-righteous religious dignitaries. She weeps over His feet and dries her tears from them with her hair. He does not embarrass her or rebuke her. What loving instinct He must have possessed to see into her repentant soul!
—See the woman with a "female disease." Following Jesus, she

reaches out and touches the hem of His robe. He turns to her when she touches Him and calls her "Daughter."

He also allowed three women (Joanna, Susanna, and Magdalene) to travel with Him and serve Him. Many other women, their names unknown to us, advanced His public ministry through their husbands' financial means.

I can't imagine Christ cracking a mother-in-law joke or farmer's-daughter joke, leering at passing women from the street corner, glancing through obscene magazines, or putting women in inferior positions. His parables are full of female prototypes—the importunate widow, the housewife who has lost one of her ten coins, the widow who places everything she has in the Temple treasury. He alludes to women in His teaching and refers to historical women as sermon illustrations—Lot's wife, a negative illustration; the Queen of the South, a positive example of faith. In His chauvinistic society, He takes up a women's cause by insisting that a man is not to divorce his wife and take another wife; He is angry at men's capricious power and consequent female degradation. He is the champion for women who have been subservient to men.

"Who are my mother, and who are my brothers?" He asks. "Here are my mother and my brothers! For whoever does the will of my Father in heaven is my brother, and sister, and mother" (Mt. 12:48-50, RSV). Based on this example, the Church must struggle to develop a new kind of community, a family of the household of faith, which expects men to treat "older women like mothers, younger women like sisters, in all purity" (I Tim. 5:2, RSV).

Many men in the Church who do not hold to Christ's standard for women are going to have to answer the question He posed in Mark 14:6. A woman came to anoint His feet and was reproached. But Jesus said, "Let her alone; why do you trouble her?" J. B. Phillips's paraphrase of this passage reads this way: "Let her alone, why must you make her feel uncomfortable?" Thinking in the context of the battered wife, the abused child, or the victim of incest, there are times when I want to fall at the feet of this Man, grab the hem of His garment, and kiss it.

A Call for the Church to Act

Scripture clearly teaches that reconciliation is the ideal for every damaged or broken relationship. In Greek, the language in which the New Testament was written, one word for *reconcile* implies "to change mutually." The Church must maintain concern for all aspects of the vicious cycle of abuse—the victim, the perpetrator, the affected marriage, and the children. We must lovingly work for reconciliation, for "mutual change."

I've heard stories of fathers refusing to be reconciled with violated family members. One father who was confronted by his adult daughter about an incestuous past said, "I'm not sorry for anything I did to my children."

I've also heard stories of confrontation which have been full of tears, forgiveness, and redemption. I want to repeat the conversation I wrote about earlier in this book that a young woman shared with me recently. Her stepfather who had molested her was also sexually abused as a child. She said, "He wept before me and confessed his sin to God. I have great hope for him. But I also know, that through my actions, I am breaking the cycle of sexual abuse. This is a condition that through the power of Christ, I am not going to allow to continue in my own family."

The Church must offer Christ's healing power in supportive, loving communities. We need holy men and women, empowered by Christ, who are not afraid to walk into the hellish lives of the abused so that victims, as well as abusers, can be set free. This kind of redemptive work will not only help individuals, but can also challenge society to alter the climate that has been nurturing abusive behavior.

Christ challenged us to be salt and light in our world. One individual in an unhealthy family who becomes whole can positively influence the rest; one small group in the church, taking on the trauma and dynamics of abuse in our culture, can educate the whole congregation and call them to action. One church in one community can set an example of righteous intervention. This chain of intervention can go on.

We must begin where we are, using the tools at our disposal, empowered by the living Christ, to influence society for good.

A cardboard box sits in my study as I work on this project. It is filled to the brim with letters from abuse victims. It is a container of pain, but it is also a source of testimony of victory. One letter, reprinted with permission from its writer gives a glimpse of that real pain and victory. It is one of several hundred which I keep to remind me of the suffering of this world and to stimulate me to be faithful in intercessory prayer.

Dear Karen,

At the time that your radio program was aired I was sitting my volunteer shift on the crisis line of our countywide hot line for rape and battering.

What you and your guests had to say really struck home. You see, for 33 years I kept silent the fact that I had been sexually, physically, and emotionally abused from the time I can remember until I was eight.

For the first 12 years of my life I was raised by my grandparents. My sexual abuse came from their neighbor and friend next door. My early memories of my mother, who didn't live with us, were that whenever it was "discipline time," she would beat me.

I grew up hating myself and blaming myself. I thought that I must have been evil. Before the age of 21 I had tried suicide twice. I did marry a wonderful man and we have two beautiful children. But until three years ago, the memories and pain of the sexual abuse influenced my life completely.

For example: When the children were younger I wouldn't let them go to friends' or relatives' homes without me because I had this continual vision that they were locked in a room, naked and screaming. Once they were nine it was easier for me to let them go, because I wasn't abused after age eight. So my fear for them started to decrease.

As a mother I wanted my children to have a "religious" upbringing. I worked on committees and taught Sunday School. I guess I was trying to "work" myself clean in the eyes of God. As you know, abused children feel very dirty and shameful. I trusted no one. I couldn't trust the word *love*.

The Lord allowed that for a while. Then He said, "No more," and for the next two years the Lord and Satan waged a battle within me.

I was afraid to trust the Lord, and Satan kept reminding me what my (now dead) abuser had instilled in me by the age of six: "No one will love you if you tell. They will blame you and send you away." I was now 39 years old, and that fear of letting go was about to literally kill me. I developed heart problems and I became partially paralyzed on my left side. I became housebound and then bedridden.

And the Lord kept saying, "Let go."

Finally, when I thought my time on earth was getting to its end, I decided to try to make some peace with God. For 33 years I had felt that I was to blame for my abuse and I couldn't get over the feeling of being unclean. I shared with a very dear Christian friend the root of my pain. She hugged me and said that it wasn't my fault.

She introduced me to a friend of hers who had been an incest victim and we did a lot of sharing. Soon I regained the usage of my left side, and within a month I was being weaned off my heart medication.

I have written several journals as part of my therapy and I hope someday to write a book—not for money or glory for myself, but to tell other women that my way of dealing with my pain was to try suicide twice. My Lord's way of dealing with my pain was to die for me once.

As a hot line volunteer, I speak to groups on what it's like to be a victim/survivor. But my greatest joy is when the opportunity comes when I can tell my audiences how the Lord gave me my life back and the healing that He has done in me.

And who better to give it all up to than the gentle Jesus who also was abused by mankind?

Sometimes it's hard to stop running and to look into His wonderful face, just as we are, dirty and scarred. But that's the way He wants us. Only then can the miracle show. His Light must first be seen through the darkness, so we new children of His can recognize it in any situation.

Thank you for telling us that He loves us and that we are special to Him.

This is our task. God, help us.

CHAPTER 7

LAWS

VICTIMS OF ABUSE AND THE ABUSERS ARE IN DESPERATE need of help. In many cases, help comes only through outside intervention. Abuse specialists have told me that situations of domestic violence and incest frequently require someone to press legal charges against the abuser before help is obtained.

Legal Protection for Battered Wives

In each of the 50 United States, it is against the law for a husband to beat his wife. Most states have a Domestic Protection Law, but legal options for battered wives vary from state to state. The strengths and weaknesses of existing laws vary greatly. These variations extend to ways the laws are interpreted and the judgments passed on the abusers. Variations can even be found within a state—from county to county.

A task force on abuse or concerned workers in the local church will have to determine what legal options are valid in their area so they can be adequately prepared to intervene in abusive situations.

For example, I phoned two shelters in DuPage County, Illinois. One was a battered wife shelter; the other was a youth and family intervention program. I was told that a battered wife can get an order of protection through the shelter which is free (not including $50 court cost), through an attorney, which can cost up to $500, or directly through the state attorney's office.

Two legal options are available to a battered wife. The first level is an "in-house order." After a court appearance, the wife is granted an Order of Protection. This order informs her spouse that, if there is another incident of abuse, she will press charges, and he will be removed from the home. The couple can still live together, but she can call the police to have him removed if he threatens, beats, or abuses her again. Some social workers feel that this is a poor option because it requires the wife to be abused

99

before it can be activated. It is an "after the fact" option. One worker told me of a woman who had an in-house protection order but was kicked down three flights of stairs before she could call police. This order is a beginning step for some women.

The second level of protection is an "exclusive possession order" which can be in effect for two years. Under this order, the woman stays in the home with the children, but the husband is not allowed on the property. The wife may receive child support and often keeps possession of the car.

As an example of intrastate legal variation, this second level of protection is not available in Chicago. There battered wives must file criminal charges against their husbands, asking for convictions carrying penalties that include jail sentences.

As a Christian helper, it is important for you to get legal counsel before the trauma of a battering incident. Pastors and Christian workers should encourage women to be informed about their legal options. "Pastors," one worker said, "should strongly encourage battered wives to get legal help, because really, until this is put into action, nothing else will help."

This may seem an extreme approach to those unfamiliar with the violence and psychodynamics of abusive families, but it is the approach our counseling staff at the Chapel of the Air uses when dealing with battered wives. Gratefully, we have seen healing and growth among couples who have come for help. We have learned that strong deterrents are often necessary to correct equally strong abuses.

Legal restraints must be combined with counseling which integrates spiritual and psychological health. The couple is encouraged to become active in a local church. Everything possible is done to save the marriage; but *first*, the wife and the children are protected by all available means.

Legal Protection for Abused Children

Child abuse is also against the law in every state in the United States. In order for intervention to take place, it is necessary to identify abuse or neglect of children. A statute for reporting abuse has been enacted by each state. In most states, some, if not all, certified or registered professionals can have their legal authorization suspended or taken away if they fail to report incidents of child abuse. Certified teachers and licensed physicians, as well as other professionals, are listed as mandated reporters. Interested child workers should check requirements in their states to see who is included in mandated professions.

As part of this legal requirement, at least one statewide agency has been designated to receive and investigate all such reports. Agencies which deal with child abuse are most likely listed under the following titles in your telephone directory:

Department of Child Protective Services
Department of Social Services
Public Social Services Department
Department of Protective Services
Social and Rehabilitative Services
Bureau of Children and Family Services

Children's Village, U.S.A. provides a toll-free national hot-line number and will gladly assist in reporting child abuse. That number is 1-800-4-A-CHILD.

A copy of local laws related to child abuse can be obtained through your local department of social services, city or county attorney's office, law enforcement agencies, or the state attorney general's office. This information should be made available to every church and lay worker who deals with children and teens.

To stop child abuse will require efforts of the entire community. Everyone must work together—parents, educators, social workers, law enforcement personnel, clergy, and legislators.

It can be emotionally difficult to actually report an incident of child abuse or neglect. If the reporter keeps in mind that he or she may be the only person who suspects the problem, that can be an encouragement to act as an advocate for that child.

Dealing with child abuse is a delicate proposition. There is often an underlying fear that the situation may have been misread or that exposure may panic the abuser resulting in more injury to the child.

Reporting child neglect can be more difficult than reporting abuse or battering because it is a "judgment call"—no bruises, cuts, or broken bones. In some states, there are no legal guidelines for supervising children. Children can be left unattended without time or age limits so long as no harm comes to the children or they don't get into trouble. Sensitivity, tact, and gentle assertiveness must be part of the child-worker's approach.

Here are some questions that workers involved with incidents of child abuse might have.

When do I report child abuse?

By law, parents must meet the "minimum needs" of their children. For example, the Illinois mandate on reporting requires that a person report *suspected* abuse and neglect. That means, upon suspicion or confirmation of some type of abuse, a phone call must be made to the proper agency. The person making the report needs to understand that he or she is protected from civil and criminal court action when the child abuse report is made in good faith. This means that there must be an honest belief or suspicion that a child is being abused and/or neglected in some way. The call can be made anonymously. The caller is not encouraged to be part of the confrontation with the parents. The caller's identity is kept confidential, and the person is immune from lawsuit even if it turns out there is no evidence of abuse or neglect.

What do I say when I make a report?

The following information should be included:
1. The name of the victim.
2. The current location of the victim.
3. The type of abuse being reported, injuries you may have noted, signs of neglect, or things that may have led you to suspect sexual molestation.

It is the responsibility of trained authorities to determine what has occurred and to what degree. In the state of Illinois, a child abuse case begins as a civil case in juvenile court. This court is concerned with protection of the child and makes no provision for penalizing the offending parent. If the situation is severe enough to go to criminal court, the penalty imposed on the parent depends if the offense is a misdemeanor or a felony. Misdemeanors are punishable by probation, fines, or up to a year in jail. Felonies are punishable by probation or time in the state penitentiary.

What happens when I report child abuse?

When one of the designated agencies receives a report of child abuse, an investigation follows in order to determine whether or not the child has been abused. At that time a determination is made as to whether or not the child is in a life-threatening environment.

Depending on the legalities of the state, procedure for follow-up is established by codes and social services agendas. Should the child be removed from the home, a decision is made regarding services that need to be provided for family members.

A plan for intervention and therapy is vital for the health and survival of the victim's family. Proper resources and experienced caseworkers are needed to deal with the many problems present in an abusive environment. In situations where abuse has been severe and long-term or where the parents are uncooperative, the case may need to be referred to the courts to protect the victim.

This reporting system is not without problems. Stephen Chapman, writing in the *Chicago Tribune* (August 14, 1983) warns, "If you are a parent living in Illinois . . . on the basis of nothing more than an anonymous phone call by someone falsely accusing you of child abuse, your home and your children may be subjected to the most invasive kind of search by agents of the state government." He reminds readers of the constitutional guarantee against "unreasonable searches and seizures" and that police cannot even enter your home without a warrant.

Chapman's article refers to a suit filed in Hammond, Indiana. The Porter County Welfare Department was accused of violating the rights of a 6-year-old child, his brother, and his parents. The legal action charged that county welfare workers improperly removed Chad Walters from his home on November 2, 1982. The suit said that a complaint of possible child abuse was filed on the basis of a reddish mark under the boy's eye after the child told school officials his mother had struck him.

The suit contended that two caseworkers went to the family home and "repeatedly and falsely accused Rhonda Walters of being a child abuser and informed her that she would not regain custody of the children until she underwent psychiatric counseling, parenting programs and other remedial actions." The social workers removed Chad and his brother from the parents' custody under an emergency verbal court order.

Two days later a judge conducted a detention hearing and brought judgment that the brother be returned to the parents and Chad be examined by a doctor. Upon obtaining the physicians report, a court order was issued stating that no evidence existed to indicate that Chad had been abused. The boy was immediately returned to his parents.

The suit contended that the small red mark under Chad's eye "was insufficient to create a reasonable inference that his physical and mental health was seriously endangered'' and alleged violation of the family's civil rights. The family sought $250,000 in compensatory damages and $250,000 in punitive damages.

Although anonymous reporting of abuse is allowed, these reports may be unreliable—only 23 percent are substantiated. This may be because no corroborating evidence is required from teachers, relatives, or neighbors. A parent has the right to refuse entry to the investigator, insisting that the caseworker obtain a warrant, to insist that the child be examined by a doctor, and to call a lawyer to inquire about his or her own rights.

On his national broadcast, psychologist James Dobson, aired a week of programs on child abuse. Many parents responded to the programs by writing about their experiences of being reported to agencies because they believed that ''sparing the rod would spoil the child.'' In too many cases, the child abuse protection agencies have become abusive themselves in regard to parent rights and violation of family sanctity. Some social workers impose their own child rearing philosophies on healthy families.

In many ways, ours is an unfortunate society. The magnitude of the problem of abuse affects all elements of society—the innocent as well as the guilty. It is imperative that the Church and Christians become informed and begin to set parameters within their communities to help so that intervention will come from a Christian ethic and not just a humanistic one.

How can I become involved in child abuse detection and prevention in my local community?

Volunteers are essential if overloaded social and legal systems are to intervene and function as advocates for the abused child and the abusive adult. Concerned individuals can help by:
1. Locating services and programs which now exist.
2. Contacting local law enforcement agencies to learn what is being done related to child abuse.
3. Become familiar with information related to child abuse prevention and treatment.
4. Volunteer time and abilities to aid in development of local child abuse prevention and treatment programs.

Legal Protection Against Incest

There are several pieces of federal legislation that allow for legal intervention when child sexual abuse occurs. In 1978, the

United States Congress amended the Child Abuse Prevention and Treatment Act to include "sexual abuse or exploitation . . . by a person who is responsible for the child's welfare. . . ." This put incest within the parameters of regulations for child abuse and neglect.

The federal law dealing with sexual exploitation of children, the Protection of Children against Sexual Exploitation Act of 1977 (18 U.S.C., Sections 2251-2253), is designed to combat child pornography. This law addresses two aspects of child abuse. It established standards for penalties to be imposed on child abusers and producers of child pornography. It also focuses on legal ramifications of the production, sale, and distribution of obscene or sexually explicit materials involving children under 16. In addition, the Mann Act of 1948 (18 U.S.C. Section 2423), which was originally enacted to prohibit the transportation of girls under the age of 18 for the purpose of prostitution, has now been extended to include boys.

In July, 1982, the U.S. Supreme Court ruled unanimously on a landmark decision that encourages sweeping curbs on child pornography. Justice Byron White wrote: "The prevention of sexual exploitation and abuse of children constitutes a government objective of surpassing importance."

Because of the growing awareness of child sexual abuse, national media coverage has disclosed the fact that most states have loopholes in their incest and rape statutes if the victim is a child. The juvenile court system has begun to be tightened to insure protection for the child as well as prosecution for the violator. Formerly prosecution had to occur in criminal court.

The Church is a sleeping giant that needs to be aroused to help, correct, and prevent. There is no unit more basic to the foundation of our culture than the family. The Church must help the home withstand erosion from divorce, the injustice of abuse, and the desensitization that comes from immoral periodicals, television, and video cassettes.

We must rouse ourselves. We dare not yawn in apathy when callous maltreatment of children and women exists in the United States—"one of the most violent nations in the world." It is time to awake, become angry, become informed, and to compassionately become involved. We are called to build, to heal, to repair, to construct, to mend, and to withstand the works of that evil one whose only purpose is to "steal and kill and destroy" (John 10:10, RSV).

We must remember that "though we live in the world we are not carrying on a worldly war, for the weapons of our warfare are not worldly but have divine power to destroy strongholds" (II Cor. 10:3, 4, RSV). There is no other institution on earth that can better take on this task than the Church of the Living God—Christ's Body here on earth.

BIBLIOGRAPHY

THE FOLLOWING ARE RESOURCES THAT PROVIDE ADDITIONAL information and help for people working with all types of abuse in the family—wife battering, child abuse, and incest. Included are helping agencies, educational programs, and a bibliography of related books.

Agencies

American Association for Protecting Children
9725 East Hampden Avenue
Denver, CO 80231
(303) 695-0811

The American Association for Protecting Children has been committed to improving services for children and families for over 100 years. Its people provide national leadership through training, consultation, research, advocacy and information dissemination. Books and pamphlets are available for a nominal fee.

CHILDHELP USA
National Campaign for the Prevention of Child Abuse and Neglect
National Headquarters
Woodland Hills, CA 91370

This organization provides free literature on child abuse and advice for establishing local advocacy programs.

Clearinghouse on Child Abuse and Neglect Information
P.O. Box 1182
Washington, D.C. 20013
(301) 251-5157

National Center on Child Abuse and Neglect
Administration for Children, Youth, and Families
U.S. Department of Health and Human Services

P.O. Box 1182
Washington, DC 20013
 This government agency is a source for statistics and research information related to family abuse.

National Committee for Prevention of Child Abuse
332 South Michigan Avenue, Suite 950
Box 2866
Chicago, IL 60604-4357
(312) 663-3520
 This organization is committed to the prevention of all forms of child abuse. NCPA has 53 chapters across the country that work with prevention—strengthening existing programs and establishing new ones. They offer an information packet and prevention resources.
Cost: $2.00 includes postage.

National Council of Child Abuse and Family Violence
Plaza La Reina
6033 W. Century Boulevard
Suite 400
Los Angeles, CA 90045
(818) 914-2814
 This organization addresses domestic violence—child abuse, spouse abuse, and abuse of the elderly. Information is provided through journals, education materials, and a quarterly newsletter. They conduct regional and local training seminars for lay volunteers, and they participate in national and international conferences for professionals.

National Criminal Justice Reference Service
P.O. Box 6000
Rockville, Maryland 20850
(800) 851-3420

National Obscenity Law Center
475 Riverside Drive
New York, NY 10115
(212) 870-3208
 This law center offers legal assistance for combating obscenity and pornography in courts and government on local, state, and national levels.

Educational Materials

Bubblyonian Encounter—a play educating children about "good and bad touches." Developed by Bubblyonian Productions, this educational experience has toured the U.S. since the summer of 1980. Today it reaches audiences through troupes of actors. Staff members also direct the play for community theater groups. A videotape is available for classroom use, private viewings, and small audiences. For complete information in order to schedule this production in your area, write:
Bubblyonian Productions, Inc.
7204 West 80th Street
Overland Park, KS 66204.

FOR PRESCHOOL AND ELEMENTARY GRADES

Berry, Joy. *Danger Zones*. 1984. Waco, Tex.: Word Books.

Part of a series of books for young children to help them become aware of how to protect themselves. Here are other titles in this series: *Abuse and Neglect; Danger: A Parent's Guide; Kidnapping; Sexual Abuse*.

Kleven, Sandra L. *The Touching Problem*. Bellingham, Wash.: Coalition for Child Advocacy.

This is a one-hour program for younger children to inform them without frightening them about the problem of sexual abuse. Write:
Coalition for Child Advocacy
P.O. Box 159
Bellingham, WA 98227

Sweet, Phyllis. *Something Happened to Me*. 1981. Mother Courage Press.

Williams, Joy. *Once I Was a Little Bit Frightened*. 1980. Fargo, N.Dak.: Rape and Abuse Crisis Center of Fargo-Morehead.

Williams, Joy. *Red Flag, Green Flag People*. 1980. Fargo, N. Dak.: Rape and Abuse Crisis Center of Fargo-Morehead.

A coloring book aimed at abuse prevention by helping children distinguish between people who bring good touches and bad touches. Write:
Rape and Abuse Crisis Center of Fargo-Morehead
P.O. Box 1655
Fargo, ND 58107.

For upper elementary grades, junior and senior high:

Fay, Jennifer J., and Flerchinger, Billy Jo. *Top Secret: Sexual Assault Information for Teenagers Only.* Renton, Wash.: King County Rape Relief.

This booklet may be obtained by writing:
King County Rape Relief
305 South 43rd Street
Renton, WA 98055

Fortune, Marie M. *Sexual Abuse Prevention: A Study for Teenagers.* 1984. New York: United Church Press.

This is a five-part study course for children, ages 12-18.

Hyde, Margaret O. *Cry Softly! The Story of Child Abuse.* 1980. Philadelphia: Westminster Press.

For Adult Helpers

Fortune, Marie Marshall. *Sexual Violence: The Unmentionable Sin.* 1983. New York: Pilgrim Press.

An ordained minister and founder of a center for the prevention of sexual and domestic violence addresses the religious community on ethical and pastoral perspectives.

Gallagher, Sister Vera, with Dodds, William F. *Speaking Out, Fighting Back.* 1985. Seattle, Wash.: Madrona Publishers.

Personal experiences of women who survived childhood sexual abuse in the home.

Green, Holly Wagner. *Turning Fear to Hope.* 1984. Nashville: Thomas Nelson.

An extensive, well-developed treatment of the wife-battering syndrome, including a theological perspective.

Hancock, Maxine, and Mains, Karen. *Child Sexual Abuse: A Hope for Healing.* 1987. Wheaton, Ill.: Harold Shaw Publishers.

A book addressed to the adult survivor of abuse, and the concerned friend, spouse, or Christian worker who wants to help. Included are steps toward emotional and spiritual health.

Herman, J. L., and Hirschman, Lisa. *Father-Daughter Incest.* 1984. Cambridge, Mass.: Harvard University Press.

Holder, Wayne M., editor. *Sexual Abuse of Children: Implications for Treatment.* 1983. Englewood, Colo.: American Humane Association.

A book for professionals or those seriously interested in the subject. To order, write:
American Humane Association
5351 South Roslyn Street
Englewood, CO 80111.

Hyde, Margaret O. *Sexual Abuse: Let's Talk About It*. 1984. Philadelphia: Westminster Press.
An easy-reading approach to the topic of sexual abuse.

Jackson, Dave. *Scared, but Not Too Scared (To Think)*. 1985. Elgin, Ill.: David C. Cook Publishing Co.
Helps parents guide children regarding safety. Teaches children to cope with frightening situations—fire, being lost, and molestation—without panicking.

Janssen, Martha. *Silent Scream*. 1983. Philadelphia: Fortress Press.
Poems about incest written by a incest survivor.

Miller, Kathy C. *Out of Control: A Christian Parent's Victorious Struggle Over Child Abuse*. Waco, Tex.: Word Books.

O'Brien, Shirley. *We Can! Combat Child Sexual Abuse*. 1982. Tucson, Ariz.: College of Agriculture, University of Arizona.
Deals with the history of child abuse, its definitions, statistics, myths, characteristics, and telltale signs.

O'Brien, Shirley. *Child Pornography*. 1983. Des Moines, Ia.: Kendall/Hunt Publishing.
A child development specialist examines the existence, prevalence, and influence of child pornography.

Olson, Esther Lee, and Petersen, Kenneth. *No Place to Hide*. 1982. Wheaton, Ill.: Tyndale House.
A case study of wife battering. Suggestions included to help the battered wife help herself.

Peters, David B. *A Betrayal of Innocence: What Everyone Should Know About Child Sexual Abuse*. 1986. Waco, Tex.:
A family counselor addresses parents of children who may have been victimized. Also helpful for those who wish to prevent the problem.

Quinn, P. E. *Cry Out*. Nashville: Abingdon Press.
A personal account of child abuse.

Ricks, Chip. *Carol's Story*. 1981. Wheaton, Ill.: Tyndale House.

The true story of an incest victim.

Trainor, Cynthia Mohr, Editor. *The Dilemma of Child Neglect: Identification and Treatment*. 1983. Englewood, Colo.: American Humane Association.

A book for helping professionals

VanVonderen, Jeffrey. *Good News for the Chemically Dependent*. 1985. Nashville: Thomas Nelson.

A certified chemical-dependency practitioner develops models by which families can help free loved ones from the bonds of addiction. For information regarding seminars conducted by the author—"Good News for the Chemically Dependent"—write:
Jeff VanVonderen
c/o Damascus, Inc.
P.O. Box 22432
Minneapolis, MN 55432